Elements in Translation and Interpreting
edited by
Kirsten Malmkjær
University of Leicester

AN EXTRAORDINARY CHINESE TRANSLATION OF HOLOCAUST TESTIMONY

Meiyuan Zhao
Peking University

Shaftesbury Road, Cambridge CB2 8EA, United Kingdom

One Liberty Plaza, 20th Floor, New York, NY 10006, USA

477 Williamstown Road, Port Melbourne, VIC 3207, Australia

314–321, 3rd Floor, Plot 3, Splendor Forum, Jasola District Centre, New Delhi – 110025, India

103 Penang Road, #05–06/07, Visioncrest Commercial, Singapore 238467

Cambridge University Press is part of Cambridge University Press & Assessment, a department of the University of Cambridge.

We share the University's mission to contribute to society through the pursuit of education, learning and research at the highest international levels of excellence.

www.cambridge.org
Information on this title: www.cambridge.org/9781009549868

DOI: 10.1017/9781009549844

© Meiyuan Zhao 2024

This publication is in copyright. Subject to statutory exception and to the provisions of relevant collective licensing agreements, no reproduction of any part may take place without the written permission of Cambridge University Press & Assessment.

When citing this work, please include a reference to the DOI 10.1017/9781009549844

First published 2024

A catalogue record for this publication is available from the British Library.

ISBN 978-1-009-54986-8 Hardback
ISBN 978-1-009-54988-2 Paperback
ISSN 2633-6480 (online)
ISSN 2633-6472 (print)

Cambridge University Press & Assessment has no responsibility for the persistence or accuracy of URLs for external or third-party internet websites referred to in this publication and does not guarantee that any content on such websites is, or will remain, accurate or appropriate.

An Extraordinary Chinese Translation of Holocaust Testimony

Elements in Translation and Interpreting

DOI: 10.1017/9781009549844
First published online: December 2024

Meiyuan Zhao
Peking University

Author for correspondence: Meiyuan Zhao, zhaomeiyuan@pku.edu.cn

Abstract: This Element focuses on two Holocaust testimonies translated into Chinese by translator, Gao Shan. They deserve attention for the highly unorthodox approach Gao adopted and the substantial alterations he made to the original texts. The Element begins by narrating the circumstances that led to these translations, then goes on to explore Gao's views on translation, his style, additions to the original accounts, and the affective dynamics of his translation activity. It draws on concepts from sociology, memory studies, and sociolinguistics to frame the discussion and highlight the ethical concerns inevitably involved in Gao's work. Without minimizing the moral responsibility of faithful transmission Holocaust material should always impose, the author wants to show how Gao sometimes sacrifices strict accuracy in his desire to make the survivors' experiences intelligible to a prospective audience unacquainted with the Holocaust.

Keywords: Holocaust, testimony, Chinese, translation, stance

© Meiyuan Zhao 2024

ISBNs: 9781009549868 (HB), 9781009549882 (PB), 9781009549844 (OC)
ISSNs: 2633-6480 (online), 2633-6472 (print)

Contents

Introduction 1

1 Story: Two Authors, One Translator 6

2 Footing: Gao's Views on Translation 14

3 Style: Readability and Elegance 21

4 Presence: The Translator as Secondary Witness 30

5 Affect: The Translator's Stance in a Triangle Model 39

    Conclusion: Out of the Ordinary 52

    References 62

Introduction

My personal translating journey began in 2020, when I translated into Chinese the autobiographical novel *Motherhood* by Canadian writer Sheila Heti. The book describes how a woman grapples with modern existential anxieties as she considers whether to become a mother in her late thirties. Translating it proved emotionally demanding. Throughout the process, I found myself perturbed and melancholic, mirroring the protagonist's inner turmoil as she wrestled with thoughts on the conditions and societal pressures bearing down on women. Her relentless exploration and struggles resonated.

Coincidentally, I learned about the publisher's expectations for the translator of this novel from a senior translator who had recommended me for the project. I was told the publisher preferred a female translator over a male, because they believed a woman could better comprehend the bodily experiences of the female protagonist, particularly on a subject as intimate as motherhood. In our current thought climate, we have become increasingly wary of anything resembling essentialism. And although at first glance such a belief might appear essentialist, it also touches on what current epistemology still sees as one of the "incorrigibles" – the notion of particular kinds of pain or (more generally) bodily experiences such as menstrual cycle and pregnancy as well as the psychosocial pressure on modern women trying to balance maternity against career aspiration. No doubt, too, the publisher's preference was connected to an awareness of the relatively conventional gender concepts still prevailing in China. So we might view the publisher's wish as rooted in the notion that empathizing with a work's content is crucial to producing a high-quality translation. Moreover, translating Sheila Heti's book turned out to be, for me, a deeply emotional journey, stirring my curiosity about the role of affect in translation.

In June 2022, when I arrived at University College London for a one-year research program, I initially contemplated a project centered around affect and translation. Delving into relevant research, however, I stumbled onto Peter Davies' monograph *Witness Between Languages: The Translation of Holocaust Testimonies in Context* (2018). It became clear that feelings, emotional affinity, and empathy are integral aspects of translating Holocaust memoirs; a profound personal and emotive link between survivor and translator is frequently emphasized. Deeper exploration of this subject yielded more complex elements at play in these texts than just affect. They encompassed acts of witnessing, translators themselves appearing within the text, adherence to ethical standards, and other significant dimensions. Gradually, my focus shifted to the translation of Holocaust testimony, becoming my primary project while at UCL.

This area of research lies at the intersection of translation and Holocaust studies, an intersection deeply rooted in history: "Translation accompanied the Holocaust from the beginning" (Hermans 2022, 108). Under the oppressive rule of the Nazis, vast numbers of Jewish people were forcibly deported within and across numerous countries in Europe. Incarcerated in concentration camps, they were confronted with a formidable linguistic challenge – the imperative to understand each other. Primo Levi noted that fifteen to twenty languages were spoken in the Monowitz-Buna concentration camp (a subcamp of Auschwitz) alone (1959, 81). Based on Levi's memoirs, David Gramling posits that monolingual inmates, unable to effectively communicate in the camp's dominant languages (German and Yiddish), were less likely to survive than inmates with multilingual proficiency; the latter also showed a greater ability to later document their experiences in writing (2012, 179). Within the multilingual environment of the camps, a unique hybrid language took shape. After World War II, as Holocaust survivors began to testify through autobiography, memoir, and documentary reports, their use of camp lexicons and idioms, of complex linguistic provenance, rendered their initial texts an unwieldy amalgamation. Gramling notes that, when the testimony was written in "broken military German, *lagerzspracha*, or a mix of languages, pidgins, and dialects," it had to be "shepherded out of the translingual matrix of its production" (2012, 182) by the monolingual publication orthodoxies of the early postwar era. It was common for survivors such as David Rousset and Hans Maršálek and their editors to explain and translate the camp jargon in their accounts, adding glossaries to their testimonies to ensure comprehensibility for their readership (2012, 170–171). Consequently, before and during the publication process, these testimonies underwent complex textual manipulation, including editing, collaborative writing, linguistic standardization, and translation. Translation played a pivotal role in the early stages of preparing these texts for public consumption.

Perception of the Holocaust has been significantly molded by the publication and dissemination of survivor testimonies. As survivors recognized the imperative of preserving their harrowing experiences for future generations, the translation of these accounts into numerous languages became a means of perpetuating their memories. While camp memoirs have multilingual roots, they depend on translation for international dissemination. It is through their translations that the works of Elie Wiesel, Primo Levi, and many others have become influential and canonical. Most readers rely on translation for their knowledge of the Holocaust. Translation has consequently played a vital part in the formation and establishment of the Holocaust corpus.

For a long time, Holocaust scholars took translated texts for granted, operating on the assumption that they were essentially identical to the original. Recent years however have seen a growing awareness of translation as something more complex, never a purely transparent, mechanical act, and this has prompted an array of new issues to come to the fore in Holocaust studies. To explore the role of translation in constructing its history, scholars like Peter Davies and Sharon Deane-Cox have drawn on memory studies and ethics as well as history and translation, working across many languages.

While some Holocaust testimonies have been translated into Chinese, serious academic study has yet to focus on these translations. The Diary of Anne Frank, a small part of which was translated and published in a Chinese magazine as early as 1959, has now seen more than a hundred new translations and adaptations. The works of Elie Wiesel, Primo Levi, and other survivors have also made their way into China. To my knowledge, however, there is virtually no Chinese academic research focused on the translation of Holocaust testimony. A check with China National Knowledge Infrastructure (CNKI, https://oversea.cnki.net/index/), the largest Chinese academic online platform, yielded nothing on the subject. I did discover roughly a dozen Chinese articles on Holocaust testimonial literature, but none seriously investigates the issue of translation. A recently published article examines the introduction and reception of Anne Frank's diary in China, reviewing the diverse translations and adaptations of the diary produced in the Chinese context since 1989, primarily through the perspective of children's literature (Zhang 2024). I also found several MA dissertations on the Chinese translation of Anne Frank's diary. One (by Dai Wanru at Chang Jung Christian University, 2016) compares several translations made by mainland China translators and translators in Taiwan. Apart from these, I am not aware of any Chinese critical or scholarly studies on the translation of Holocaust testimony.

My research concerns the Chinese translation of two Holocaust testimonies: Max Stern's autobiography *My Stamp on Life* (Melbourne, 2003) and his cousin Olga Horak's *Auschwitz to Australia: A Holocaust Survivor's Memoir* (Sydney, 2000). Written in English, they were both translated by Gao Shan and published in China – Stern's in 2004 and Horak in 2010. Gao's translations count among the earliest Holocaust survivor memoirs translated into Chinese. They are also striking in the remarkable liberties taken by the translator. The primary objective of my study is to document and try to understand this unusual feature of the translator's work. To do this, I will draw on concepts from sociology, memory studies, and sociolinguistics.

I chose Gao Shan's translations for several reasons. First, they are among the earliest Chinese translations of Holocaust memoirs. To my knowledge, just over twenty now exist in book form in China. Before the publication of Max Stern's autobiography, only five such testimonies had appeared in Chinese. I also found that only seven of the twenty-odd testimonies were by female witnesses. Of these, Olga Horak's *Auschwitz to Australia* marked the first testimony authored by a female survivor translated into Chinese.

Second, Gao is a nonprofessional translator who found an unlikely publisher for his translations. His official job concerned the international postage stamp trade, where he met and then established a close personal connection with Max Stern. It was through friendship that Gao was entrusted with the task of translating both Stern's and Horak's books. Gao further used his philatelic connections to place the works with a publisher specializing in stamps. These circumstances render Gao's translations exceptional in the broader landscape of Holocaust memoir transmission, but their most intriguing attribute lies in the extraordinary liberties he takes. Typically, both survivors, such as Primo Levi, and scholars, such as Sharon Deane-Cox, insist on strict textual accuracy in the translation of Holocaust testimony. The liberties Gao takes stand in direct contrast to these principles.

Third, as a translator, Gao provides a uniquely Chinese perspective on the Holocaust. While Western scholars emphasize the Holocaust's unparalleled place in human history, the paratexts accompanying Gao's translations draw attention to the Japanese invasion of China in World War II and the horrific atrocities committed during that period. In his effort to make the remote and foreign events of the European Holocaust intelligibile to Chinese readers, Gao seems to suggest a parallel in the Japanese atrocities, still one of the most traumatic collective memories for the Chinese people.

During the course of my research, I had the privilege of personally communicating with the translator, Gao Shan, as well as Olga Horak, and some of Max Stern's descendants. In August 2022, I submitted a written questionnaire to Gao Shan, and was fortunate to find him highly cooperative, providing insightful answers to my inquiries. He generously shared a number of materials that immensely enhanced my understanding of various details, from his comments on the events surrounding his translation production to his email exchanges with author Max Stern and other friends on the topic of translation.

The present Element consists of five sections. Section 1 narrates the genesis of Gao's translations. Section 2 deals with Gao's views on translation as illustrated in the paratexts, that is, the various supplementary texts accompanying his translations. Sections 3–5 are analytical, each concentrating on distinct textual aspects of the two translations.

In a finer-grained outline, we begin with Section 1, where I introduce the three central figures of my study: Max Stern, Olga Horak, and Gao Shan. I give an overview of the life experiences and writings of the two authors. This section also offers contextual details about the translator, including his personal acquaintance with the authors, his career as an official in the China National Philatelic Corporation, the publishing history of his translations (issued by the Posts and Telecom Press, a publishing house previously under the purview of the China Ministry of Posts and Telecommunications, which also oversaw the postal corporation where Gao was employed), and his efforts to promote these translations.

Section 2 looks at the paratextual materials accompanying the translations, including Gao's prefaces and afterwords, as well as his answers to the questionnaire I sent him in 2022, his comments on events surrounding the publication, his email exchanges with Max Stern and other friends, and some reader reviews. I indicate how Gao, by invoking the renowned Chinese translator Yan Fu, clearly prioritizes readability and elegance over verbal accuracy in his translations. Furthermore, I explore how he reconciles his pursuit of stylistic refinement with the original authors' noticeably rougher writing style.

Section 3 presents textual examples demonstrating Gao's efforts to make his translations both readable and elegant. Regarding readability, I tease out the methods he adopts in translating German, Hebrew, and other references in the originals, showing his intent to lighten the burden of comprehension for target readers unfamiliar with these terms and concepts. With respect to elegance, I highlight Gao's additions of idioms and phrases, scenery descriptions, and reflections on the Holocaust as his attempts to render the works more refined and to his mind profound. I draw on Pierre Bourdieu's concept of *habitus* to explain these interventions, arguing that Gao transfers his professional modus operandi as a high-ranking company official to his work as an amateur translator.

Section 4 investigates Gao's presence in the translated text by drawing on the idea of secondary witness. As understood in memory studies, the secondary witness is a sympathetic listener who facilitates the Holocaust survivor's testimony. Following Sharon Deane-Cox's lead in considering Holocaust testimony translation a form of secondary witnessing, I demonstrate how, in the paratexts accompanying his translations, Gao is keen to show his bonding and intimate connection with his authors, drawing on his own experiences and comparing the suffering of the Chinese people under Japanese invasion to Nazi persecution of the Jews. For the same reason, his translations make substantial additions to the source texts. Gao clearly assumed his role as secondary witness in a highly personal way, and employed radical means to make his witnessing as effective as possible.

In Section 5, I apply sociolinguistic theories of stance-taking – in particular the stance triangle model created by John W. Du Bois (2007) and modified by S. F. Kiesling et al. (2018) – to analyze the affective aspects of Gao's translations.

The model offers three dimensions, namely, *affect*, *investment*, and *alignment*, for analyzing a speaker's stance: through their evaluation of a certain object (*affect*), the intensity of that evaluation (*investment*), and how it aligns or does not align with the views of other participants in conversational exchange (*alignment*). The model enables me to investigate how, in his desire to serve as a secondary witness, Gao amplifies particular instances of suffering under Nazi rule, and why he reshapes scenes of family life in the original texts, along the lines of Chinese audience stereotypes. Additionally, I examine cases where, under pressure from his publisher, he downplays the misdeeds committed by Russian soldiers.

My conclusion focuses on the ethical issues raised by Gao's translations. In his striving for effective dissemination and reception of the survivors' Holocaust testimony, Gao unquestionably sacrifices textual accuracy. I discuss how, in this engagement of translation with Holocaust writing, we discover a tension between the putative ideal of preserving the original's integrity and the possibility of actually achieving that ideal. Gao's perspective on translation theory and his actual practice only heighten this tension. They present an uncommon, perhaps even extreme case, highlighting not only the ethical concerns surrounding the translation of Holocaust testimony but also the significance of its broader sociocultural context.

1 Story: Two Authors, One Translator

Gao Shan was not a professional translator, nor did he have any special interest in or knowledge of the Holocaust before he set out to translate the works of Max Stern and Olga Horak. His official job was that of a manager in a state-owned postal service company in China. However, between 2003 and 2011, he used his spare time to translate three works written by two Holocaust survivors. This section provides overlapping stories of the two survivors' lives and writings, as well as details about the translator.

1.1 Max Stern

Max Stern (1921–2016) was born into a middle-class Jewish family in Bratislava, then part of Czechoslovakia, as the eldest of seven children. His interest in postage stamps at the age of twelve spurred a lifetime career of stamp collecting and dealing. In the early stages of World War II, his family was protected from deportation because of his father's job listing books confiscated from the Jews for the Nazis. But with Hitler's "Final Solution," the family was torn apart, and his parents and two youngest brothers were captured and gassed at Auschwitz. Stern went into hiding but was finally caught and sent to the concentration camps. His worst experience of camp life was in Sachsenhausen, a labor camp in Oranienburg, Germany, where he arrived in early 1945. Sachsenhausen was not an extermination camp, but Stern suffered doing forced labor under inhumane conditions. He was then sent to Lichtenrade, one of the satellites of Sachsenhausen on the outskirts of Berlin. In April 1945, as Germany was losing the war, the camp was evacuated and all were marched out. Stern set out on the "death march" together with other prisoners, until one day in May, the SS guards were gone and the prisoners became free. On March 2, 1948, his 27th birthday, he married another Jewish survivor, Eva Rosenthal. With the political situation worsening in postwar Czechoslovakia, the couple soon made plans to leave Europe. They arrived in Melbourne, Australia, in July 1948 and built a new life there.

Stern developed his stamp-collecting hobby as a young boy. When war broke out, he had to abandon his engineering studies and work instead in the stamp-dealing business to support his family. The contacts he made through trading stamps protected him during the early years of the war. After moving to Melbourne, he gradually built a stamp empire, his company becoming one of the world's best known stamp dealers. His experience of the Holocaust and with postage stamps figured among the most influential factors shaping his life.

Stern wrote two memoirs: *My Stamp on Life*, published by Makor Jewish Community Library in Melbourne in 2003, and *The Max Factor: My Life as A Stamp Dealer*, also published by Makor, in 2011. Both describe his early life in Bratislava, his survival of the Holocaust, and his stamp-trading career in Australia, but they are different in the extent to which they relate the Holocaust. While *My Stamp on Life* tells Stern's life story with the War and the Holocaust as key events, *The Max Factor* is mostly about the author's entrepreneurial career in philately, with only the occasional background reference to the Holocaust. *My Stamp on Life* was issued in Makor's "Write Your Story" collection, and included in Monash University's Holocaust Autobiographies Catalogue, a database of over 180 memoirs written by survivors of the Holocaust and published in Australia.[1] A publisher specializing in Judaica, Makor promoted both Stern's Holocaust narrative and his achievements in the stamp-dealing world. They published *My Stamp on Life* as the memoir of a Holocaust survivor who developed his stamp business, and *The Max Factor* as the first history of philately in Australia from 1948 to the present day. Since the second book does not have much to do with the Holocaust, my project will focus primarily on *My Stamp on Life*.

---

[1] Website: www.monash.edu/arts/acjc/research-and-projects/online-resources-and-mini-sites/holocaust-memoirs#S

1.2 Olga Horak

Born Olga Rosenberger in Bratislava on August 11, 1926, Olga Horak (1926–) is Stern's cousin.[2] When war broke out in 1939, she was a young girl emotionally unprepared for the horror unleashed on her and her family. Suffering increasing hardship, the family fled to Hungary, but as the situation worsened there as well, they returned home. In 1944, they were deported from a friend's house in Bratislava to the transit camp Sered, one of the main collection points for Slovakian Jews. From there they were sent to Auschwitz-Birkenau. Olga saw how the notorious Dr. Joseph Mengele, the "Angel of Death," chose prisoners to conduct experiments on, and witnessed the SS carrying out their systematic killing in the camp's gas chambers. Later she and her mother were transported to Kurzbach, one of the subcamps of Gross Rosen concentration camp, and became part of a forced labor unit. Around Christmas 1944, they started the "death march" toward Gross Rosen, Dresden, and Bergen-Belsen. They were finally rescued from Bergen-Belsen by the British army.

Both Olga's father and her elder sister were murdered during the Holocaust. She and her mother survived the camps, but her mother died just moments after being registered on the day of Liberation, leaving Olga the sole survivor of her family. On February 9, 1947, she married another Holocaust survivor, John Horak, and the couple emigrated to Australia in September 1949, establishing themselves in Sydney. They built the Hibodress blouse factory and their products became very popular in Australia. Olga Horak's memoir, *Auschwitz to Australia*, published by Kangaroo Press in Sydney in 2000, is a testimony describing her suffering and healing. It depicts a young girl maturing into womanhood during and after the Holocaust. Like *My Stamp on Life,* Horak's work is included in the Holocaust Autobiographies Catalogue.

Olga Horak's memoir had as editorial adviser Paul O'Shea, an Australian theologian, educator, and historian whose research focuses on Catholic responses to the Holocaust. He taught for many years in Sydney's Catholic schools and authored monographs *A Cross Too Heavy: Eugenio Pacelli, Politics, and the Jews of Europe, 1917–1943* (Rosenberg Publishing, 2008) and *A Cross Too Heavy: Pope Pius XII and the Jews of Europe* (Palgrave Macmillan, 2011) on the actions and policies of Pope Pius XII (Eugenio Pacelli) regarding the Holocaust. Given that his research closely relates to European Jewry and the Holocaust, O'Shea was well-suited to edit Horak's book. In his foreword, he states that he kept Horak's story and voice as they originally were, limiting his task to suggestions for clarity and accuracy of details (O'Shea 2000, xii).

---

[2] Stern's mother is the younger sister of Horak's father.

O'Shea also makes a comment on Horak's lack of formal education and rough writing style. According to Horak, her school life had been interrupted for four years, roughly from the age of fifteen to nineteen, due to Nazi persecution; after the war, her request to go back to school was denied and she had to get a job. O'Shea's idea seems to be that while Horak's writing style is different from that of other writers, her own voice had to be kept intact. He suggested that instead of weakening her testimony, her style will remind readers of "the awful power wielded by those who engineered and executed the 'Final Solution'" (O'Shea 2000, xii).

1.3 Gao Shan

Gao Shan (1958–) is a former high-ranking official at the China National Philatelic Corporation in Beijing, which is affiliated to China Post Group Corporation. He retired as General Manager of the Stamp Distribution Department in 2019, and is now living in his home city, Shenyang in Liaoning Province, in northeast China. I contacted him on August 22, 2022, and we have kept in touch ever since. I initially sent him a questionnaire, asking how he came to translate Holocaust testimony and found a publisher for them. We have never met in person, all our communications taking place via WeChat messages, but he is unfailingly supportive and has responded to all my inquiries.

1.3.1 The Translation of My Stamp on Life

Gao was born into an educated family in Beijing in 1958, both parents being intellectuals. In 1979, he entered the Department of Foreign Languages at Liaoning University. He studied English literature, and, after graduation, was assigned a job at the International Office of the China National Philatelic Corporation. There he worked on the import and export trade of stamps, and was charged with managing their Australian clients. In the 1980s, Gao became acquainted with Max Stern through the business dealings between China and Australia. They maintained a friendship of nearly three decades, until Stern's death in 2016.

In 1992, Gao was learning business management at MDM Wholesale, an international stamp and coin trading company, in Braunschweig, Germany. It was at a stamp exhibition in Essen where Gao was engaged in MDM's practical sales service that he met Stern and first learned of his Jewish identity. In May 1998, Israel Post hosted an international stamp exhibition in Tel Aviv, which brought together stamp-issuing directors, including Gao, from all over the world. During the exhibition, Stern invited the directors to visit Yad Vashem, the famous Holocaust memorial in Jerusalem. On the way there, he sat next to

Gao and told him about the loss of his family to the Holocaust and the memoir he was writing. His story touched Gao deeply and Gao agreed to have Stern's memoir translated into Chinese.

Four years later, when Stern published *My Stamp on Life* in English, Gao was struggling in his own career. The first half of Gao's working life had gone smoothly enough: He had joined China National Philatelic Corporation when he was twenty-five, and after about a dozen years, at the young age of thirty-eight, he had climbed all the way up to deputy General Manager. Then, in December 2002, things went wrong. He was held jointly liable for some malpractice concerning the employees' insurance and received an administrative warning. Although he felt he had been misunderstood and treated unfairly, he was "exiled" to a postal printing company, Beijing Hongna Post Products Company, a place where retirees were sent and there was little to do. Gao's low spirits caught Stern's attention. Stern visited him in Beijing and suggested that, instead of abandoning himself to despair, he should find something positive to do, like translating Stern's recently published memoir. Gao readily took the advice.

Gao finished the translation and quickly secured its publication with Posts and Telecom Press, a large professional publishing house established in 1953 and previously under the purview of China's Ministry of Posts and Telecommunications. Given the nature of the company, Holocaust testimony was hardly one of their key interests. Nonetheless, Gao turned to them because the publisher belonged to the same postal system in which he himself worked and they had, in fact, just published his own first monograph, *Selections of Philatelic Research* (《邮话连篇》 2004). The editors at the Press were familiar faces to him.

As Max Stern was a household name in international stamp dealing, the Press was more than happy to publish his memoir. Gao was aware that the editor-in-chief appreciated the book as an account of a career in philately, rather than a personal Holocaust experience, so he gave the parts concerning stamps more prominence. He asked Stern to add a chapter exclusively for the Chinese edition, relating his connection with China Post and his sales of Chinese stamps in Australia. The translation of *My Stamp on Life* was published in October 2004.

1.3.2 The Translation of Auschwitz to Australia

After the translation of Stern's memoir, Gao's career was still at a low ebb. Stern suggested he continue translating Holocaust testimonies, this time the memoir of his cousin Olga Horak, *Auschwitz to Australia*. Through Stern's connections, Horak soon authorized Gao to translate her book. In early 2005, during a trip from Melbourne to Poland for the 60th anniversary of the liberation of Auschwitz,

Stern stopped in Beijing and presented Gao with a copy of Horak's memoir. He told Gao the memoir was a sensation in Australia and a German edition was in preparation.[3]

By October 2005, Gao had almost finished the draft translation, but he lost the manuscript during a business trip. It was on a train journey to Shenyang when he was asked to undergo a security check but inadvertently left his manuscript behind. When he recovered it two months later, it arrived with a letter from the head of the train crew. According to his self-introduction in the letter, this train conductor graduated from a rail technology college in 2000 and was employed in the Shenyang railway section. He explained that he happened to see Gao's draft and was deeply touched by it. He recalled that earlier that year, during the Spring Festival holiday, he and his new wife took a trip to Europe, where they visited the Dachau concentration camp near Munich. This experience caused him to respond with emotion to Horak's memoir. He praised the translator's command of the Chinese language and expressed his delight that someone in China was translating a book documenting Holocaust history. This commentary is quoted in full in Gao's afterword to the translation.

The publication of this translation, however, was not easy. Unlike the Stern book, Horak's memoir has no connection to stamps; it focuses entirely on the subject of the Holocaust. Hence, Gao struggled to persuade the Posts and Telecom Press to publish it. He even tried other publishers outside his immediate circle, approaching Masses Publishing House who considered it but turned him down in the end. Frustrated, he posted part of his translation on a website called "House of Good Books" and put the full manuscript on a back burner. Two developments would later rekindle his interest. First, in December 2008, he learned from the internet that there had been five Chinese victims in the Mauthausen concentration camp in Austria.[4] It is now known that, for racial or ideological reasons, Chinese people were detained in several Nazi concentration camps but the topic is largely neglected by Chinese historians (Zhang 2021). Gao himself was surprised to learn that some of his own countrymen were among the Holocaust's victims. Then, in January 2009, Gao received a phone call from a China Central Television director who wanted to get in touch with Max Stern. They knew about Stern's Holocaust experience from Gao's previous translation of the Stern book, *My Stamp on Life*, and they hoped

---

[3] The German edition later appeared in 2007, published by Hartung-Gorrre in Konstanz.
[4] In November 2002, Professor Wolfgang Johannes Bandion, board member of the Austrian camp community Mauthausen, found among its materials registration records of five Chinese killed in the camp. He delivered the relevant files to the Chinese Embassy in Austria. In May 2003, led by the Chinese government, a memorial plaque was dedicated to the Chinese nationals who perished in the Mauthausen concentration camp (Li 2005).

to invite the author to their upcoming commemoration of the 65th anniversary of the liberation of Auschwitz. Later that year, on August 12, Gao also received an email from Stern, telling him of a plaque at Mauthausen commemorating the Chinese who had been murdered there – something Stern had not been aware of.

These events reminded Gao of his translation manuscript of Horak's memoir which had been laid aside for several years. He checked the website "House of Good Books" and found many reviews expressing a wish to see the complete translation published in book form.[5] He then took the manuscript to the Posts and Telecom Press again, negotiated with them, and finally obtained their approval to publish it. Notably, during the manuscript's delay, Gao's career took a turn for the better. In March 2006, he was transferred from Hongna to the leading position of the newly established China Post Advertising Company. In persuading the Posts and Telecom Press to bring out Horak's memoir, Gao's prominent position in the postal industry no doubt played a part, but he also adjusted the original to please the publisher. He inserted the story of Rowland Hill inventing the modern stamp into Horak's narration and added introductions to Max Stern and his achievements in the stamp business. He rephrased these passages in the original to make his additions look natural. The translation of *Auschwitz to Australia* was published in January 2010, in time for the 65th anniversary of the liberation of Auschwitz, and as a companion piece to the Chinese translation of *My Stamp on Life*.

1.3.3 Book Events

Gao pushed for book launch events to boost the translations. Organized by the Posts and Telecom Press and official philately institutions, they captured the attention of state-run news media. Max Stern attended the event for *My Stamp on Life*, held on October 29, 2004 at the Traders Hotel in Beijing, and gave a speech (see Figure 1). But Gao chose not to attend because on the podium were people he felt had made false charges against him in his former company. Even though Stern urged him to attend, Gao refused to share the stage with them.

The event for Olga Horak's memoir took place on January 27, 2010, at the National Hotel in Beijing. This time Gao was there, but Olga Horak was unable to attend. She made a video appearance to convey her greetings to Chinese readers and remind them that history must not repeat itself. The Australian Embassy in China thought highly of the Chinese translation and sent their Deputy Head of Mission, Graeme Meehan, to give a speech (see Figure 2).

---

[5] This is stated by Gao in his afterword to *Auschwitz to Australia*. I also asked him personally and gained his confirmation on this. Unfortunately, I have not been able to find any trace of the website in question.

Chinese Translation of a Holocaust Testimony   13

Figure 1 Max Stern at the launch of the translation of *My Stamp on Life*, with interpreter Wu Di

Figure 2 At the launch of the translation of *Auschwitz to Australia*: (left to right) Jiang Wei, Deputy Director of Posts and Telecom Press, Graeme Meehan, Deputy Head of Mission, Australian Embassy, Beijing, and Gao Shan

The publisher printed and distributed 3,000 copies of Max Stern's memoir and 2,500 copies of Olga Horak's. I have not found much information regarding sales, but Gao noted in the questionnaire that the Chinese translation of *My Stamp on Life* sold out quickly and was reprinted in 2011 in 800 copies, mainly because Stern wanted to sell them in his Melbourne stamp shop.

In 2011, Gao's translation of Stern's other book, *The Max Factor: My Life as A Stamp Dealer*, was published, also by Posts and Telecom Press. Gao used the book, primarily about the stamp business, as practical training material for employees in his company as it apparently worked quite well. Its launch took place in conjunction with the Asian Stamp Exhibition Philatelic Seminar on November 13, 2011, in Wuxi, Jiangsu Province. Stern attended the event and gave a speech. Although this book has little to do with Holocaust, the event made Stern, as both stamp dealer and Holocaust survivor, more widely known to Chinese readers. Copies of the Chinese translation of *My Stamp on Life* were also sold at its event, which marked the last time Stern visited China and met with Gao.

The works by Max Stern and Olga Horak are the only books Gao ever translated. In the next section, I will consider Gao's self-positioning as a translator and the way his translations were received by Chinese readers.

2 Footing: Gao's Views on Translation

This section tackles the consciously crafted scaffolding for Gao's translations, that is, the paratexts that accompany and adorn his main translation texts. Following Gérard Genette, I distinguish between peritexts, which are physically attached to the main text and appear together with it, and epitexts, which tend to be at some remove from the main text (Genette 1997, 4–5; Batchelor 2018, 12). They indicate the way Gao approached his task and steered his reader in a certain direction.

The peritexts are Gao's prefaces and afterwords. All of his three translated texts feature both, offering crucial space for Gao to express his motivations, aims, and expectations as translator. His preface to *My Stamp on Life* introduces his friend Max Stern to the Chinese reader. It details Stern's engagements with China as a globally recognized stamp dealer, his experiences during the Holocaust, and how Gao came to translate Stern's memoir. The afterword describes the book's significance both for the development of philately in China and for encouraging the anti-fascist spirit of the Chinese people. In his preface and afterword to *Auschwitz to Australia*, Gao presents his reflections on the Holocaust and narrates several anecdotes from the process of getting the translation published. Although the third book, *The Max Factor*, is mostly about stamp exchange, Gao's preface and afterword are particularly valuable in revealing his general thoughts on translation as well as what Stern shared with him about his writing.

The epitexts are of different kinds and result from my communication with the translator in 2022. First, there are Gao's answers to the questions I put to him – on his translations and writings, his dealings with Max Stern and Olga Horak, and the publication of his translations. I sent the questionnaire to Gao on August 22, 2022 and received his answers on the same day. Between August 25 and 29, Gao forwarded to me his email exchanges with Stern talking about the publication and launch events for the translations, and with his friends discussing translation issues. These emails yield insights into Gao's close relationship with Stern, as well as his decision-making process in translation. On September 4, 7, and 10, respectively, Gao offered me commentaries, all prepared in the form of essays, on each of his translations in which he recounted his experiences with translation, particularly as they correlated with his career development in the stamp world. Last but not least, I have collected a small number of newspaper notices and reader reviews from the internet, which shows a general picture of the testimonies' reception in China.

2.1 Yan Fu's *Xin, Da,* and *Ya*

In his afterword to *My Stamp on Life*, Gao describes how he took Yan Fu's three criteria of translation to heart:

> …… 我在大学读书时，翻译老师的第一堂课就讲了中国思想启蒙运动的先驱严复先生在其译著《天演论》中提出过著名的翻译三原则："信、达、雅"。可以说，从一百多年前起，中国的很多翻译工作者已经将此三原则奉为指导他们翻译工作的金科玉律，我在翻译这本书时也不例外。
>
> [... when I was a student at university, the first lesson of my translation teacher was on the famous three criteria of translation, "faithfulness, expressiveness, and elegance" put forward by Yan Fu, pioneer of the Chinese enlightenment movement, in his translation of [Huxley's] *Evolution and Ethics* [or *Tianyanlun*]. It can be said that, for more than a hundred years, many translators in China have followed these three criteria as a golden rule to guide their translation work, and I am no exception in translating this book.][6] (Gao 2004c, 149)

Yan Fu (1854–1921) was an educator and translator, famous for introducing China to the Western ideas of Thomas Huxley, Adam Smith, John Stuart Mill, and Herbert Spencer. In his preface to his 1898 translation of Huxley's *Evolution and Ethics*, Yan proposed the three challenging criteria of good translation, *xin* (fidelity), *da* (fluency), and *ya* (elegance).[7] These would become the gold standard

---

[6] The bracketed English translation, here and throughout, is by the Element author, unless otherwise indicated.

[7] The three terms have been variously rendered in English: *xin* can be translated as faithfulness, fidelity, and trueness; *da* as comprehensibility, expressiveness, intelligibility, readability, and

widely pursued and admired in Chinese academic circles. *Xin* literally means being true, honest, and faithful to the original text; *da* conveys expressiveness, accessibility, and getting through; and *ya* comprises the educated, refined quality, and beauty of a language. Both *da* and *ya* cater to a smooth, enjoyable reading experience. "The fundamental tenets of twentieth-century Chinese translation theory" (Chan 2004, 4), these criteria have shaped an enduring paradigm in the field of Chinese translation.

Gao sought to channel Yan Fu's translation principles into his work. He described this in some detail with Zhang Yuliang, an old college friend who had emigrated to Australia. In September 2010, Yuliang managed to buy a copy of Gao's translation of *Auschwitz to Australia* at the Sydney Jewish Museum. An email discussion followed in which Gao voiced his thoughts on translation:

> 我信奉严复先生提出的翻译要"信达雅",其实,这三个标准,我个人最看重雅……我的翻译观是:我不需要忠诚于单词,也不需要忠诚于句式,我要忠诚的只是意思,就是作者想要表达的信息。
>
> ……最好不能让别人一眼就看出来是翻译文章,不能让读者阅读的流畅感受到影响。如果是作者文字水平一般、逻辑感不强,我也要通过译文对原文进行修正,否则读者骂的肯定是译者而不是作者。因此,我想英译汉的精髓在于汉语,而不是英语。
>
> [I believe in Yan Fu's three principles of translation: *xin*, *da*, and *ya*. In fact, I personally attach the greatest importance to *ya*. ... This is my view of translation: I don't need to be faithful to words, nor to syntax, just to the meaning, that is, to the message the author wants to express.
>
> ... It's best not to make anyone feel, at a glance, that it's a translated work—you can't undermine its natural fluidity. If the author is not good at writing and has a poor sense of logic, I have to improve the original in my translation; otherwise the target reader will definitely scold the translator rather than the author. Therefore, I think the essence of English-to-Chinese translation lies in Chinese, not English.] (October 29 or 30, 2010)

Even as he shows his high regard for Yan Fu's three criteria, Gao indicates his personal priority is the fluency of his translations. He privileges their style and elegance over literal fidelity while still conveying the *meaning* of the originals. Since neither Stern nor Horak is a native speaker of English or a great stylist in writing, Gao's translations would have to improve on their books. Gao quotes Stern's casual attitude to autobiographical writing in his preface to *The Max Factor*: "Autobiographies do not have to care too much about literariness; they only need to express genuine feelings" (Gao 2011a). As for Horak, we have in

---

fluency; and *ya* as elegance, refinement, and gracefulness. See the table of English translations of Yan Fu's terms in Hermans (2014b, 143–144).

Paul O'Shea's foreword to the original book, comments on her interrupted education and his intentionally limited linguistic assistance to improve Horak's writing, both highlighting Horak's own, presumably plainer style. All of this begs the question, how does Gao reconcile his own desire for elegance with the originals' lack of refinement?

2.2 Elegance vs Roughness

Since Gao cites Stern's casual approach to autobiographical writing and clearly reads O'Shea's foreword to Horak's memoir, we know he was fully aware of the roughness of the originals. But unlike O'Shea who considers the survivor's plain writing valuable evidence of the impact the Nazi regime had on her education, Gao decides to enhance and refine the original texts to create better books for his readers. Explaining his approach in his afterword to *The Max Factor*, Gao first shares how Stern explicitly granted him a free hand in his translations:

> 最令我欣喜并让我踏实的是，老人在信中说，翻译时不一定拘泥原文，在不影响书中表达意思的前提下，可以小作调整。

> [What delighted me and put my mind at ease the most is that the old man [Stern] told me in his letter: it is not necessary to stick to the original text when translating; minor adjustments can be made as long as they don't affect the meaning expressed in the book.] (Gao 2011b, 193)

With the author's permissive attitude in mind, Gao appears to have felt entitled to prioritize the transmission of the original's overall meaning rather than its words or syntax. He went on to describe his method of translation:

> 翻译书籍，会情不自禁地走进作者的世界中，笨拙地或自以为聪明地把自己"翻译期待"的假设与已知的文字相替换，这也就是翻译书时步入的一个境界: 丰富原文。其实,这在翻译界也是惯常的景象。的确，有些"假如"的构想也实在是诱人呵。有了一番"假如",它或许会比没有"假如"更加逼近真实的原文。
>
> 这就是我追求的翻译方法……

> [When translating a book, one cannot help but go into the author's world, clumsily or, acting on the strength of one's own imagined cleverness, replacing the original texts with one's assumptions or "translation expectations." That is the state one steps into when translating: enriching the original. Actually, it is a common thing in the field of translation. Some "what if" ideas are really tempting. With those ideas, it [the translation] may be closer to the true original than it would be without them.
>
> This is the method of translation I pursued...] (Gao 2011b, 193)

Gao conveys a robust confidence in this approach. He believed that by enriching the original he was better able to stay "true" to it. He threw himself into the work, on top of a heavy workload at his day job. He later recalled his state of mind when translating:

> ……挑灯夜战、废寝忘食不算，还常常放下笔后久久不能入睡，有点儿走火入魔的意思。
>
> [... not only did I work through the night and forget to eat or sleep, but I also couldn't sleep for a long time after putting down the pen, being a bit carried away.] (Gao 2011b, 194)

This is how Gao identified with his authors, stepped into their mental world, and put his own ideas into the originals. The statements were made in his paratext to *The Max Factor*, but it is the same approach he brought to the previous two translations. He neglected Yan Fu's criterion of fidelity and pursued "elegance" and refinement by altering the original texts wherever he felt this was necessary. In translating O'Shea's foreword to *Auschwitz to Australia*, Gao omitted O'Shea's analysis of Horak's rough style and inserted his own reflections on Horak's extraordinary personality in the face of the Holocaust, emphasizing the severity of the hardships she underwent, the indelible imprint they left on her life, and her resilience and diligence. He hoped to bring to his target audience an elevating and didactic book, assuming that the historical lessons and spiritual encouragement were what readers should get from reading Horak's life story.

It's important to note that Gao was not providing a translation service like most professional translators do. His strong grip on the books originated in his relationship with the authors, especially with Stern, which we can glimpse from Stern's side as well. When the Chinese translation of *Auschwitz to Australia* was published, Gao sent a copy of it, and later a DVD of the book launch, to Stern. Stern replied by email to Gao:

> I will certainly make sure that this book will be displayed along with my own book you translated in both the Melbourne and Sydney Museums. I hope that you will one day honour us with your visit and see for yourself. Thank you again for everything. I treasure our friendship. (January 14, 2010)
>
> Many thanks for the DVD of Olga's book launch. It is really beautiful and you have gone through a lot of trouble for which both Olga and myself will be forever grateful. (March 1, 2010)

In two subsequent emails conveying greetings, Stern said to Gao:

> Whenever we talk about China your name comes up first – my personal relationship with you of nearly 3 decades has been enjoyable and apart from

our business dealings your personal friendship is greatly appreciated. The 2 books you translated for me are part of the unforgettable times of the past. (December 22, 2014)

 If I am still alive, you are on the top of my list for my 100th Birthday. (February 5, 2016)

These emails highlight the value Stern placed on his friendship with Gao. He was clearly aware of the challenges Gao faced in making the testimonies available to Chinese readers, and he emphasized his gratitude for Gao's crucial role in translating and securing publication for his and Horak's books in China. He took Gao as a warm-hearted and capable friend who was doing him a favor in bringing their Holocaust stories to broader audiences. Unlike in many cases where translators find themselves in an inferior position, Gao felt no such pressure from the authors; he was not a translator servant who expected to work gingerly for the author master; instead, he and the authors were friends and collaborators on an equal footing. This may have led Gao to feel justified in following a translation style that suited his own mind.

However, Gao signaled his approach only in the afterword to his third translation (of *The Max Factor*), not the two testimonies. In the afterword to *My Stamp on Life*, he said he followed Yan Fu's *xin-da-ya* as the golden rule guiding his translation, but he did not mention his preference for two of them (with, as a correlative, neglect of the third). He voiced his principle of aiming at faithfulness to the overall meaning (rather than word-for-word or sentence-for-sentence) and his privileging of readability and elegance over strict verbal accuracy only in a private email to a friend. This means that he gives no indication of his unorthodox method to the general readership of the two testimonies.

2.3 Reader Reviews

Reader reviews can play a paramount role as platforms for accessing a translated text. Apart from the train conductor's letter accompanying the return of Gao's lost manuscript discussed in Section 1, there are a few short essays reviewing Gao's translations, the most important being two news reports appearing in *People's Daily* on January 9, 2005 and March 19, 2010, both by the journalist Yuan Xi. *People's Daily* represents the official voice of the Chinese central government and is the most influential and authoritative daily newspaper in contemporary China. These reports reviewed the Chinese translation of *My Stamp on Life* and *Auschwitz to Australia*, taking them as commemorative publications for the 60th and 65th, respectively anniversaries of victory in the global war against fascism and of the liberation of Auschwitz. They affirm the value of both books in preserving Holocaust survivors' memories and passing on the historical lessons drawn from the Holocaust, thus preventing genocide and other serious crimes, and promoting a culture of peace across the world.

I also found two short commentaries on the Chinese translation of *My Stamp on Life* and nine short commentaries on *Auschwitz to Australia* on Douban.com, a popular online book platform in China. For the first book, the reviews revealed readers' surprise at Stern's legendary life experience. One reader expressed astonishment that Stern's "hobby and work in stamp collection could be so useful in helping him escape Nazi persecution" (Anonymous, December 6, 2007). Stern describes just that – how, in the early period of the war, his connections with the Slovak secret police through stamp dealing helped him escape arrest. His stamp trade also generated foreign exchange for the government, which exempted him from deportation. All of this increased his chances of survival. Many Chinese readers were drawn to Stern's autobiography because of their own passion for collecting and selling postage stamps, and they appreciated the role of philately in Stern's wartime struggles. For the second book, basically, all the reviews describe the readers' shock at Nazi cruelty and their sympathy for the Jewish victims. For example, one reader wrote "[through this book] I keenly felt the suffering endured by the Jews subjected to Nazi persecution" (Anonymous, February 22, 2012).

Nearly all the reviews of the two translations that I have seen concern the lessons of the Holocaust; no one compares the books with their originals. Of course, most Chinese readers do not have access to the foreign original and can only comment from the target side. However, I saw a special review from Yuliang, who lived in Australia and had managed to read both the original and the translation of the Horak book. In an email to Gao on October 31, 2010, he made the following comments:

> 达与雅被你运用的如此自如，绝非初出茅庐之辈，令我感动又佩服。你忽略了信，可是你的忽略成就了一本好书。作为一本自传体裁的书籍，如果没有你的提炼，读者读起来恐怕不会有如此大的冲击。
>
> 但我始终还是坚持译文首先要做到信，为此才能正确地转达原作者的意图。那我又为什么说你的译著好呐，那是因为撰写自传的作者并非都是作家，因而对某些事情认识得并非那么深刻，故此需要译者的再创作。

[You accomplished *da* and *ya* exceptionally well. It wouldn't be expected from anyone but an expert, and I'm truly impressed. You neglected *xin*; but your neglect resulted in a remarkable book. I fear that without your refinement, the autobiography would not have had such a profound impact on the readers.

I still insist the translation must be faithful to accurately convey the author's intentions. But I think your translation is great because not all autobiography authors are good at writing or are able to offer insightful observations. Some works need to be reworked by the translator.]

Yuliang's admiration for Gao's proficiency with Yan Fu's *da* and *ya* does not preclude his noticing Gao's neglect of *xin* and the unfaithfulness of his translation. Nonetheless, Yuliang justifies this shortcoming by pointing out the necessity of sometimes improving the original's unpolished writing style. He agrees with Gao that translators should actively engage in reshaping a text to enhance the reader's overall comprehension of it and acknowledges the value of Gao's alterations in making the essence of the books more accessible to target readers.

This section has shown how Gao fashioned himself in the role of translator. Various paratextual materials illustrate how he invokes Yan Fu's three criteria of translation while putting his own personal interpretation on them, how he reconciles this standard with the original textual reality, and the kinds of responses he gets from readers. He privileges fluency and elegance at the expense of fidelity; by virtue of his friendship with the authors, he determines to refine the originals with genuine devotion; and his translations seem to enjoy a largely positive reception. However, as Genette stresses at the end of his monograph, paratexts are "only an assistant, only an accessory of the text" (1997, 410); the meaning of a translated text depends on the translation itself, rather than on the discourse around it. Hence, the following sections will cross the threshold and examine the actual translations.

3 Style: Readability and Elegance

Gao champions fluency and elegance, sometimes at the expense of fidelity. His take on Yan Fu's three translation criteria leads him to his own linguistic style as translator. In this section, I will document Gao's efforts to make his translations both readable and elegant. Regarding readability, I identify the methods he employs to translate various German and Jewish cultural references in the originals; these methods reveal his intention to ease the burden of comprehension for his target readers. As for elegance, I analyze the significant additions Gao makes, apparently in an effort to deepen, strengthen, and dignify the key message of the memoirs. I then draw on Pierre Bourdieu's concept of "habitus" to further contextualize these latter interventions.

3.1 Readability

I find Gao's intention to increase his translations' accessibility especially evident in the way he tackles various foreign, culture-specific items – words and phrases that refer to historical events, Jewish customs, or camp life in German, Yiddish, Slovak, and other foreign languages, appearing in both Stern's and Horak's books. The difficulty in translating items of this kind usually emerges through "denotative or connotative lacunae" (Bodeker 1991, 65), or the discrepancy in information between the original and the target lexicons. Leaving these items untranslated or unexplained in translations may pose a problem for the reader if they are restricted to the source culture, and either nonexistent or bearing a different intertextual status in the receiving environment.

Academic discussions that provide substantial or serviceable guidelines for translating information-loaded terms tend to be scarce. In a 1996 article, Javier Franco Aixelá published a systematic survey of the various strategies to render culture-specific terms. Translators, he suggests, have a number of options, "ranging from conservation (acceptance of the difference by means of the reproduction of the cultural signs in the source text) to naturalization (transformation of the other into a cultural replica)" (Aixelá 1996, 54). His discussion gives us a glimpse of translators' concerns in treating the source text, particularly their wish to maintain readability. Following Aixelá, I will tease out Gao's renderings of the original items and divide them into four categories. Instead of attempting a complete presentation of all such translations here, I intend to select a couple of typical examples to illustrate my classification of the methods Gao adopts.

Gao's first method is to translate a term literally and then add a note at the bottom of the page to explain its implications. The supplementary explanation is put in the form of footnotes, distinguished from the main text to avoid illegitimate mixture. For example, the Nazi word "KAPO" (Horak 2000, 38) was transliterated into Chinese characters on the basis of phonetic similarity, "卡波" (Horak 2010, 43), and Gao's note explains it refers to a prisoner functionary assigned by the SS to supervise forced labor in the concentration camps.

In Gao's translation of *My Stamp on Life*, there are thirty-five translator's notes in total. Of these, twenty-two concern people, places, historical events, or organizations concerning the Holocaust, the Second World War or European history; seven have to do with Jewish languages and culture; three are related to stamps, letters, or numismatics; two are concerned with Australian history; and one, at the beginning of the Chapter "China—A New Experience," informs the reader that this chapter was written by Stern exclusively for the Chinese translation of the book. In the Chinese version of *Auschwitz to Australia*, there are altogether forty-seven translator's notes, of which thirty-three are about people, places, historical events, or laws concerning the Holocaust, World War II or European culture; eight are about Jewish language and culture; five are about Australian culture or history; and one is on the "Mohawk" hairstyle (named after a native American people) in which a concentration camp guard shaved a woman (as humiliation) to punish her for stealing bread. None is about stamps or letters (as the original Horak story contains next to nothing about stamps).

In addition to employing footnotes, Gao also integrates explanatory information directly into the main text, so as not to disrupt the reader's attention. For example, sometime around late September/early October 1944, Horak saw a camp as she exited the train and knew she had arrived at Birkenau. When the term "Birkenau" appears in the main text, Gao inserts a few lines of introduction to Auschwitz-Birkenau for the target reader without breaking into the original narration for too long. Translators usually maintain brevity and subtlety in their intratextual supplements. However, some of Gao's intratextual glosses are very long. An extreme example is his translation of the German term *Kindertransport*, referring to a British program to rescue Jewish children from Nazi-occupied territories just before the outbreak of World War II. Horak mentions "Kindertransport" in her memoir as a last-ditch effort of Jewish parents to save their children, though her own parents, wanting to keep the family together, decided not to send her and her sister. Gao translated the term into Chinese as "'挽救儿童'计划" ['Rescue the Children' Program] (Horak 2010, 9) and explained in an extraordinarily long gloss, six paragraphs in total, the tragic situation of Jewish children, the requirements of the British government, the number of children transported, and their lives with host families in England. Gao seemed to consider this information important for the readers to know, and thus did not limit himself to the original text, nor was he bothered by the potentially excessive length of the gloss.

In other occurrences of foreign-language terms appearing in the source texts, Gao did not supply extra information. Instead, he rendered them using techniques known as generalization and explicitation. Generalization here means the translator replaces some words and phrases with broader, more universal references. For example, "Yomim Noraim" (Stern 2003, 77), referring to the High Holy Days, strictly Juadaism's two most important holidays of Rosh Hashanah and Yom Kippur, Gao translates more generally as "犹太节" [Jewish Festival] (Stern 2004, 66). Explicitation is used to make the connotations of the original term more visible to the target readers. Elisabet Titik Murtisari, who has studied the concept, describes it as elusive, pointing out that it may include "shifts resulting in a more general expression than the corresponding [source text]" (Murtisari 2016, 68). But, I see the two concepts as distinct from each other. Whereas generalization tends to blur the source text information, explicitation clarifies it. Contrary to generalization, explicitation moves to a higher degree of specificity and particularity. For example, the "Nuremberg Laws" (Horak 2000, 1), a set of antisemitic laws enacted by the Nazis in 1935, was translated into "纽伦堡种族法" [Nuremberg Laws of Ethnicity] (Horak 2010, 3), with its ethnic aspect made explicit.

Finally, there are words and phrases that Gao just omitted and did not translate at all. Examples include "Volksdeutscher" (Stern 2003, 40), a term used by Nazis to refer to ethnic Germans living outside of Germany with no German citizenship, and "Wahrman Utca on Kresz Geza Utca" (Horak 2000, 16), the place where Horak's family rented a flat when hiding in Hungary in 1943. The omitted references are mostly names that denote certain detailed objects and have no significant connotations. Gao presumably thought of them as trivial information, not warranting the comprehension effort required of the reader, nor their loss substantially affecting readers' understanding.

Gao adopts various methods to make his translations more readable. Since notes heavy with information can hinder fluent reading, he doesn't add a note to all culture-specific items, but uses his own discrimination to grant some of his supplementary explanations as intratextual gloss, while others are concisely translated by generalization or explicitation, and still others are simply omitted, alleviating the burden of comprehension. Gao uses diverse techniques to deal with such terms because he cares about the reading experience of his target audience. As indicated by his statements on prioritizing fluency, he is committed to the role of translator as responsible mediator who makes it easier for readers to understand the message the author wishes to convey. It should be acknowledged that the multilingual nature of the authors' Auschwitz experience is lost in his translations. Culture-specific items in the originals are written mostly in non-English words. Their inclusion could give English readers an authentic sense of the historicity of the narrated events. In translation, however, they become monolingual Chinese, their foreign, polyglot characteristics erased. As a result, the translated texts become flatter than the original, and target readers cannot sense the language mixture in the originals or have a similarly layered reading experience.

3.2 Enhanced Elegance

To enhance his translations' style and make them more elegant, Gao intervenes with numerous additions – incisive summaries, comments on life and human nature, invented stories, and descriptive passages expanding on events in the originals. This is especially noticeable in the translation of Olga Horak's *Auschwitz to Australia*. In his paratexts, Gao states that he privileges readability and elegance over accuracy, but he says almost nothing about his copious additions, which are not only sizable, they are unmarked. He puts many of these additions in the author-survivor's (implied) voice. Hence, the reader without access to the original will not be able to tell which part comes solely from the translator and will thus read the entire text, including Gao's additions, as the words of the original author.

Gao's pursuit of elegance comprises two tiers of meaning. First, he refines the language, polishing his expressions until they look smooth and graceful to him. Second, he deepens the theme. He tries to see through the surface phenomena, reflect on them, and bring to the target reader what he thinks is the truth that can be extracted from the author's experience. He expects the interventions to enhance the quality of his translated texts, making them more worthwhile reads for the target reader. In this section, I will present three types of textual additions for elegance: idioms and phrases, scenery descriptions, and reflections on the Holocaust.

First, Gao polishes the original texts by adding Chinese idioms and four-character phrases. Traditional Chinese idioms are mostly four-character set expressions originating in vivid stories of Chinese culture, history, and society. As they express complicated ideas with wit and wisdom, their use demonstrates a writer's high cultural literacy and adds flavor and energy to the writing. Apart from the use of idioms, Gao invents new four-character phrases which have similar linguistic effects.

One example concerns Olga Horak's loss of the family property. After the war, when Horak returned home to see her parents' property, she was bluntly told by the Kramars family who had leased it from her parents that the place was no longer hers. They told her they were convinced its previous Jewish owners were dead, and had purchased the estate under the previous Slovakian regime. This is Horak's narration alongside Gao's translation, with Gao's additions underlined:

Original:
They had been convinced that we were all dead and no one would ever return to claim the estate so it was now theirs. I left … (Horak 2000, 98)

Translation:
理由是他们相信我们都死了，没有人会回来认购[8]那些财产，所以他们举家抢房，鸠占鹊巢。那些自己编排的故事自然都是无稽之谈，我离开了……

[The reason is that they were convinced that we were all dead and no one would ever return to claim the estate. Therefore, their entire family snatched our property, like the turtledove taking the magpie's nest. Those made up stories are of course all nonsense. I left …] (Horak 2010, 106–107)

Obviously, Horak was disappointed at the loss of her family's property, but she didn't argue and just left. Gao suggests the new owners fabricated stories to fool Horak and it was all baseless talk. He adds two strongly negative phrases: a four-character expression "举家抢房" (the whole family snatches the property) and an

---

[8] Gao inadvertently uses the wrong character; the correct phrase is "认领" (claim), not "认购" (subscribe for).

old Chinese idiom "鸠占鹊巢" (the turtledove occupies the magpie's nest)[9] to imply the seizure of another's residence by force. By using this idiom to describe the later family's occupying the estate in an arrogant and unreasonable way, Gao suggests the postwar social disorder as well as the coldness of the human heart. It seems to me that Gao made these comments because he identified with the author, was keen to speak for Horak, and thus hastened to take up the cudgels on her behalf.

Gao's additions appear not only as single-sentence idioms, but also as prolific private fantasies and thoughts filling whole paragraphs. This is a more drastic move to enhance the works' elegance. The additions are as imaginative as they are extensive, often crafted in beautiful, delicate (if sometimes corny) Chinese prose. Through his fabrications, Gao is highly skilled in making them harmonize with the given topic to fit seamlessly in the original. As an example, I will show the scenery embroidered onto Horak's narrative of moving between camps.

In the winter of 1944, Horak and her mother were sent to Kurzbach where they were made to do forced labor. While the prisoners trudged along the snowy road to their worksite, Gao added the following depiction:

> 森林是茂密的，小路蜿蜒其中，沿途偶尔可以发现树上有几只你根本不认识的鸟儿，被雪水淋透;在枝桠间，大鸟悄无声息地为小鸟梳理着羽毛，狼狈中透出无私的亲情。看着一队囚犯从眼前走过，它们侧头看着树下经过的每一个人，发出温柔的咕咕声。
>
> [It was a dense forest, with a trail weaving through it. Along the way you would spot a few birds in the trees that you couldn't even recognize. They were drenched in the melting snow. Among the branches, a large bird was quietly preening the feathers of its young, showing a selfless affection in their wretchedness. Watching a group of prisoners walking in front of them, they turned their heads, stared at each person passing under the trees, and made gentle cooing noises.] (Horak 2010, 62)

Obviously, the parent bird and its young suggest a parallel to Horak and her mother. In an effort to appreciate the female protagonist's state of mind, Gao creates this scene to imply Horak and her mother were sticking together in difficult times. The description gently intensifies the atmosphere, making the target readers more sympathetic and protective of the Jewish prisoners in their distress. Additions like this far exceed the normal remit of a translator, but they surely increase the literary flair of the translation, while possibly appearing platitudinous and hackneyed to some critical eyes.

---

[9] Magpies are famous for their bulky, durable, well-constructed nests of sticks and twigs. Despite the literal meaning of the idiom, turtle doves are usually not nest stealers. The bullying bird who tend to show interest in other birds' nests might actually be red-footed falcons or cuckoos.

In his comments on the translation of *Auschwitz to Australia* (accessed on September 7, 2022), Gao wrote that he considered it a deficiency that the author only narrated events superficially, without reflection on the nature of Nazi atrocities; he seemed to consider such reflections indispensable benefits for his target readers. For example, Horak witnessed Joseph Mengele, notoriously cruel doctor at Auschwitz, perform all kinds of hideous medical experiments on prisoners. Her memoir mentions his obscene experiments on young female prisoners, his injecting blue dye into children, and other brutal, sadistic behavior. Gao goes further in his translation, offering a comment on why the Nazis would commit such inhuman crimes:

> 其实, 奥斯威辛集中营与德国纳粹的存在就是以杀人为目的的。屠杀和死亡在那里无处不在、无时不有, 而且已经使死亡的性质发生了变化——它不再是意外的不幸和极限的来临, 而是一个日常现象和"研究"所需。
>
> [In fact, Auschwitz and the German Nazis existed for the purpose of killing. With them, massacre and death were everywhere and happened all the time; they changed the nature of death – it was no longer an unexpected misfortune and the coming of one's end, but a daily phenomenon and a necessity for "research."] (Horak 2010, 53)

The original testimony solely recounts the crimes that took place in the camp and does not delve into Nazi methods. While other translators might consider this a feature of the original's unique mode of narration and treat it as such, Gao clearly does not interpret the lack as an authorial style choice he needs to respect. Instead, he chooses to elaborate on these descriptions by summarizing the nature of the Nazis' inhuman acts, analyzing their motivations, and offering a more explicit critique of their killing systems at Auschwitz. Perhaps Gao reckons his readers would find the heinous crimes unfathomable, and with his remark on the nature of death at Auschwitz he tries to penetrate to truth. Killings became routine, common, and mechanical, at the death factory, the killers so accustomed to it that no pain could tug at their heartstrings. I believe Gao's additions, if not profound or brilliant, are unquestionably useful in supplementing the original testimonies. His additions provide general Chinese readers, who often have very little knowledge of the Holocaust, with a much stronger appreciation of the themes and significance found in Horak's memoir. Therefore, the Chinese translation does not limit itself to relating horrible surface phenomena but taps into "deeper thought" through the translator's interventions.

These additions serve to make the translated texts more elegant, albeit at the expense of fidelity to the originals. And elegance, as a criterion of Yan Fu's tripartite dictum for translation, has always been disputed among translation practitioners and scholars. It is fidelity that is usually assumed to take prominence over other requirements to guarantee a translation's credibility. Gao's huge amount of intervention goes against normal translation conventions. So why did he tailor the originals according to his personal literary taste? I turn to Pierre Bourdieu's sociological ideas for a possible interpretation.

3.3 Transference of Habitus

Pierre Bourdieu offers a model to capture the social context of translation. He formulates the concept of "habitus" as the "supra-individual dispositions capable of functioning in a ... collective way" (Bourdieu 2000, 156). According to Michaela Wolf's summary of the key concepts of Bourdieu's cultural sociology, "habitus" is the principle of perception, appreciation and action acquired by individuals through experience and socialization; it is a set of embodied dispositions naturally and durably adapted to a certain professional field (Wolf 2010, 339). Social agents have their habitus shaped by their various types of "capital," that is, the accumulated labor or disposable resources agents own or represent. Bourdieu classifies them into four types: economic capital (material possessions), social capital (networks of family members, friends, and colleagues), cultural capital (education, knowledge, etc.), and symbolic capital (prestige and social honor) (Wolf 2010, 339). The distribution of these different forms of capital is responsible for the operation of social forces.

I found Bourdieu's concepts of "habitus" and "capital" useful in interpreting Gao's bold interventions and disregard for fidelity. As a leader of a large state-owned corporation, Gao presumably received a reasonable salary and possessed enough economic capital. He had close connections with many important people in the postal business. His social capital worked quite well for the publication of his translations because he knew the directors and editors in the Posts and Telecom Press personally. He was also very knowledgeable and experienced in stamp dealings, and had published monographs on stamps and letters – he undoubtedly possessed significant cultural capital. Last but not least, by occupying the leading position at his company, he acted as a symbol of authority and thus had great symbolic capital.

Rich in the four types of capital, Gao is confident and competent in the management of stamps. He may be only an amateur in translation, but he is a big name in Chinese postal circles. Sameh Hanna points out that the hierarchy of social classes is one of the factors constituting what Bourdieu calls a "field of power," and conditions practices within the field of translation (Hanna 2016, 200).

Gao, at the top of the hierarchical order at his company, is inclined to translate the books in the same authoritative manner he displays in his stamp business. Since habitus is socialized and internalized as an unconscious disposition, I speculate Gao transfers the competence of his habitus in the stamp world to the world of translation. This might well explain why he prefers not to be constrained by the original texts and makes additions until the translated texts align with his taste. The capital Gao possesses in the stamp world grants him significant autonomy in producing his translations, just as it enables him to promote them by organizing book launch events.

Gao aims at both easier accessibility and a higher aesthetic quality of the translated texts, bringing the works up to his own standards and having them radically localized. This approach, however, raises serious ethical issues. He breaks into the originals' territory and makes drastic appropriations for himself. In this way, he becomes the de facto commentator, rewriter, and coauthor of the works by the two survivors, though what he produces is presented and perceived as translation. Fascinated by Yan Fu's tripartite *xin-da-ya* dictum, Gao may have known about Yan's way of dealing with his own fidelity challenge while translating *Evolution and Ethics*. His statement, in his preface to this work, explaining his departure from fidelity can help us understand Yan's practice. He explains his departure from fidelity as follows:

> 译文取明深义, 故词句之间, 时有所颠到附益, 不斤斤于字比句次, 而意义则不倍本文。题曰达旨, 不云笔译, 取便发挥, 实非正法。
> (Yan 1933, 1)
>
> [My translation attempts to present its profound thought. It does not follow the exact order of words and sentences of the original text but reorganizes and elaborates. However, it does not deviate from the original ideas. It is more an exposition than a translation as it seeks to elaborate–an unorthodox way of transmission.][10] (Yan 2004, 69)

Yan Fu confesses to his reader that he elaborated, paraphrased, and added to the original texts, which could explain why Gao says the translator's enrichment of the original is "a common thing in the field of translation" (Gao 2011b, 193). Instead of being submissive, he sees his role as active. Instead of delivering an identical reproduction of two Holocaust survivors' testimonies into Chinese, he aims to facilitate the understanding of the Jewish survivors' experience among Chinese readers. He endeavors to inspire, impress, and enlighten through the many additions he thinks will work for the benefit of his readers.

---

[10] C. Y. Hsu's translation.

4 Presence: The Translator as Secondary Witness

Holocaust testimony is inherently about witnessing. Survivors bear witness not only to their own suffering, but also to the indelible memory of those who perished in the Holocaust. Bearing witness to that era of history motivates documentation and memorializing of personal experience. The act of translation, as it involves receiving and transmitting survivors' stories, can also be seen as a form of bearing witness. In this section, I borrow from memory studies the idea of secondary witness to investigate Gao's presence in the translated texts.

4.1 Translator as Secondary Witness

The idea of secondary witness dates back to Dori Laub, a psychoanalyst engaged in the practical treatment of trauma survivors. Based on his own multiple roles – as child survivor of the Holocaust himself, interviewer of other survivors, and scholar researching Holocaust testimonials – he understands various perspectives and recognizes three distinct levels of witnessing: "the level of being a witness to oneself within the experience; the level of being a witness to the testimonies of others; and the level of being a witness to the process of witnessing itself" (Laub 1992b, 75). The first level arises from his own experience as a survivor as he vividly remembers his deportation, the camps, and his childhood afterwards. The second level proceeds from his participation in eliciting and forming other survivors' accounts. As the interviewer and immediate receiver of testimony, he empathetically relives and reexperiences the Holocaust together with the interviewees, and acts as a companion in their journey back to past sorrows. The third refers to the process of witnessing the narrator's and listener's process of witnessing. As a researcher, he reflects on the narrator's and listener's behavior, checks the veracity of the story, builds links to the present, and sees if they are reaching the truth. The second of Laub's three levels of witnessing is what scholars later defined as "secondary witness."

Aleida Assmann creates a dual model of witnessing comprising two roles: the primary witness has the experiencing role of one who goes through the ordeal, while the secondary witness serves a testifying role describing to others what happened in the name of those who are no longer able to speak for themselves. She then compares the religious martyr and the Holocaust witness, and points out that one of their differences lies in the separation or fusion of primary and secondary witnessing. After the martyr dies, it is up to a bystander to tell their story, hence the two layers of witnessing are separate: the martyr as the first witness (through personal experience), and the bystander as the second witness (helping describe the martyr's story to others). By contrast, these two layers are conflated in the case of the Holocaust testimony, where the person who experiences the massacre is the same who testifies to it.

Assmann insightfully suggests two points of view in which the experiencing and testifying roles can be clearly marked for the Holocaust witness. The first is to consider those who died and were forever silenced in the Holocaust as the primary witnesses, and those who were spared the worst and were able to write a testimony as the secondary witnesses who speak not for themselves but for the other dead victims. The second is to view the survivor in the role of the primary witness, and the receivers of the testimony in the role of secondary witnesses, defining the latter as the person who "listens to the testimony with empathy, and helps record, store, and transmit it" (Assmann 2006, 269). She also noted that "the secondary witness is the point of origin not of the event itself but of its story and transmission" (Assmann 2006, 269). Then, a variety of agents – recording, transcribing, translating, and communicating the testimonial stories for the survivors – may be counted as secondary witness.

Sharon Deane-Cox first recast the translator of Holocaust testimony as a secondary witness in the transmission of the survivor's memory. To her, the translator is a secondary witness because he or she "as a hermeneutic listener to and receiver of the survivor's lived experience plays a fundamental role in its reconstruction and retranslation" (2013, 311). The translator obtains knowledge of the Holocaust by listening to or reading the testimony, and witnesses for its author by retelling it to a new audience. They are one step removed from the lived experience being recounted, but play an essential and generative role in the transmission of Holocaust memory. In this way, the author of the testimony or the Holocaust survivor can be viewed as the primary witness, while the translator of the testimony, as the receiver of the survivor's testimony, can be viewed as the secondary witness.

The role of secondary witnessing puts the translator of Holocaust testimony into a more definite subject position. In interviewing survivors and enabling a testimony, the listener partakes in the victims' struggle with their traumatic past. That is to say, the secondary witness claims a full role in the translingual reconstruction of the testimony. If we follow Deane-Cox's lead and call the translator of Holocaust testimony a secondary witness, we can say that the translator is definitely entitled to claim a visible presence in the translation. The presence rather than invisibility of translators is necessarily justified in the translation of Holocaust testimony.

The concept of secondary witness is helpful in explaining Gao's method of presenting his translations to target readers, and specifically why, in the paratexts accompanying his translations, Gao both stresses his intimacy with the authors and draws a comparison between the German Nazis and the Japanese invaders of China. He engages in secondary witnessing in his translations, even if not explicitly cognizant of the role.

4.2 Intimacy with the Authors

Laub asserts that bearing witness to trauma demands "a bonding, the intimate and total presence of an *other*" (1992a, 70; italics in the original). Therefore, the translator, as secondary witness, must be there with the author, to listen to the author's story, and to be empathetically engaged with the author's narration. They need to be active in reconstituting, mediating, and transmitting the survivor's memory. For this reason, the translator tends in paratexts to prominently display their bonding and intimate connection with the author: striving to prove to readers their personal ties with the author, they demonstrating how they know them well and thus can understand them correctly. This corresponds to Peter Davies' observation that translators of Holocaust memoirs do not usually emphasize professional distance or objectivity but instead try to show their personal contact or intimate connections through family or friendship with the author. As he concisely puts it:

> No translator (of testimonies) stresses the usefulness of a position of professional distance or objectivity, even though this might be a perfectly reasonable attitude to guarantee an excellent job; instead, where it is possible, translators stress the intimacy of their connection with the author. (Davies 2018, 44–45)

In other words, translators actually *highlight* their intimate connection with the author to enhance their translation's value, despite the potential benefits of maintaining professional distance for more objectivity. As Davies shows, Elie Wiesel, in praising his wife Marion Wiesel's retranslation of *Night*, underscored that she "knows my voice and how to transmit it better than anyone else" (Wiesel 2008, xiii). He emphasized their relationship as a positive aspect of her retranslation. Closeness between translator and author of a Holocaust testimony may be seen to give a translated text an advantage.

Gao, too, stresses his intimacy with the authors, especially with Max Stern. In his preface to *My Stamp on Life*, an essay titled "Lao Ma, An Elderly Foreigner Whom I Respect," he introduces his friend Max Stern to Chinese readers. "Lao Ma" is a Chinese nickname Gao gave Stern playing on the similarity of his first name "Max" to the Chinese family name "Ma." "Lao" is an adjectival adjunct denoting familiarity, often used before an address as a term of endearment or intimacy (Lin 1972, 180). By calling Stern "Lao Ma," Gao conveys the sense of his close relationship with the author. Apart from that, since "Ma" literally means a horse, an animal symbolizing energy, health, and strength, this nickname carries positive connotations, suggesting Stern's resilience in the face of Nazi cruelty and his long-term commitment to the stamp business.

In the same preface, Gao provides a detailed account of how he came to know Stern, recounting their business meetings and shared meals. Their relation was summarized as follows:

> 二十年了，我们相处得非常好，可以说是情投意合。
>
> [For twenty years, we [Max and I] have been getting on very well and it can be said that we are closely allied in opinions and feelings.] (Gao 2004b, 2–3)

He shows the readers that they are like-minded close friends. Although his relation with Olga Horak was not as close, he still tries in his preface to *Auschwitz to Australia* to highlight his connection to her. He begins by invoking his Holocaust survivor friend Stern who suggested the translation of his cousin Olga Horak's memoir, and Horak's unreserved endorsement of his work. He lets the readers know that he was able to contact the author and consult her on any question he had while translating.

The translator's personal connection with the survivor authors is of prime importance for the translated text. By stressing this intimacy, Gao maintains a connection with the primary witnesses' experience and seeks to deliver a seamless chain of witnessing. Detailed descriptions of their interactions will enhance the credibility and authority of his translations.

4.3 Comparing Chinese Wartime Experience to the Holocaust

Bettina Stumm points out an inherent self-centeredness of secondary witnesses of the Holocaust: "Witnessing others is inescapably self-referential: I experience others for myself through my sensory perceptions and identification with them, seeing them in relation to me" (2010, 355). She suggests that "secondary witnesses are apt to assimilate the unfamiliar to that which they have experienced or can understand" (2010, 356). Often considered a bad thing, self-centeredness is also a common, inevitable phenomenon. As secondary witness, the translator of Holocaust testimony may resort to familiar sufferings from their own context in order to understand.

In witnessing for Jewish victims, Gao uses his paratexts to recall the suffering of Chinese people during the Japanese invasion of World War II, as a more familiar experience to himself and his target readers. Nazi Germany and the Empire of Japan were also military allies. Both countries were guilty of committing war crimes in neighboring countries: While Nazis murdered Jews across Europe, Japan engaged in campaigns of mass killings in conquered territories in Asia, and forced women from Korea, China, and other occupied countries into sexual slavery. The Nazi camps, in Levi's words, were "the culmination of Fascism in Europe, its most monstrous manifestation"(Levi 1987, 390), while Japan's invasion of China in 1937 marked the apex of Japanese fascism. The Holocaust and the Japanese atrocities in China may be considered crimes of fascist powers that bear some resemblance.

In his afterword to *My Stamp on Life*, Gao compares the remembrance culture in Germany and Japan after World War II:

> 和德国不同的是，与纳粹同时代的日本法西斯独裁者和大战犯 ......
> 被一些日本人当神一样供奉着 ...... 日本右翼份子竟敢篡改历史教科
> 书， 日本的一些政府领导人还多次参拜供有甲级战犯亡灵的"靖国神
> 社" ......

> [Unlike in Germany, the Japanese fascist dictators and war criminals who were contemporaries of the Nazis .. .. are [still] worshipped by some Japanese like gods .. .. The Japanese right-wingers have altered history textbooks and some Japanese government leaders have repeatedly visited the "Yasukuni Shrine" where the souls of A-Class war criminals are enshrined ...] (Gao 2004c, 152)

Here, Gao hints at praise for postwar Germany's commendable efforts to confront its role as the perpetrator in the Holocaust. They have given restitution to heirs of the victims, promoted a culture of commemoration, and increased education about the Holocaust among their youth. It seems much harder for Japan to establish a critical dialogue with their serious crimes in the past. In contrast to Germany's acknowledgment of responsibility, there is no consensus or clear position to deal with war crimes in Japan's official politics (Schmidt 2016, 1–2). Gao saw Japan's attitude toward history as opposite to Germany's responsible gesture. He condemns the Yasukuni Shrine, controversial symbol of Japan's war legacy. A Shinto shrine in Tokyo, built to commemorate Japan's soldier casualties since the Meiji Period (1868–1912), it lists among its 2.5 million dead roughly 1,000 war criminals, including 14 A-Class criminals.[11] Enshrinement of Japan's worst convicted war criminals has led to many controversies and visits by some Japanese politicians to the Shrine have damaged Japan's relations with other Asian countries such as China and South Korea.

The Chinese translation of *My Stamp on Life* was published in October 2004. I notice that Gao's afterword is dated September 18, the memorial day to the so-called 9.18 Incident or the Mukden Incident. On September 18, 1931, the Japanese Kwantung Army attacked the Manchurian city of Mukden (now Shenyang, Gao's

---

[11] A-Class criminals: some of Japan's top leaders who were tried as the worst criminals committing crimes against peace by plotting and waging war.

home city), the beginning of their invasion of all of Manchuria. An incident contrived by the Japanese army to conquer China by force, it marked the beginning of China's war of resistance against Japan's invasion. Presumably, when Gao was preparing the afterword, he was affected by this special memorial date, and recalled Japan in his reflections on the Holocaust.

The connection may have been prompted more broadly by international relations in the early 2000s, when a wave of anti-Japanese public mobilization swept across China (Reilly 2012, 99–100). In 2001, Japan's Ministry of Education authorized a new conservative history textbook for use in schools. The textbook downplayed the nature of Japan's military aggression in the wars invading China and South Korea, sparking anti-Japanese sentiment in Chinese media and society. At the time of Gao's translation work, roughly 2003 to 2005, Japan's Prime Minister Junichiro Koizumi visited the Shrine annually, despite protests from the Chinese Foreign Ministry.

Hence my speculation is that when Gao was working on the translations, contemporary international events likely spurred his comments on the sharp contrast between Germany's and Japan's repentance for their history of invasion. In his preface to the Chinese translation of *Auschwitz to Australia*, Gao quotes Stern on the central importance of this history:

> 他对我说，二战期间，德国法西斯主义和日本军国主义都对人类犯下了累累罪行。如果人们不熟知那段历史，就无法理解20世纪是怎么回事。
>
> [He [Stern] told me that during World War II, both German fascism and Japanese militarism committed a lot of crimes against humanity. If people are not familiar with that history, they cannot understand what the 20th century was all about.] (Gao 2010a)

Though Gao quotes Stern for the parallel between Germany and Japan, it seems to represent his own view as well. When his translation of Olga Horak's book was reviewed in *People's Daily* shortly after, Gao shared a relevant personal experience:

> 译者高山说："中华民族与犹太民族一样，在第二次世界大战中惨遭践踏……"高山告诉我：他小时候曾在辽宁阜新生活过一段时间，亲眼见过当时发现的日寇侵华时屠杀中国劳工的万人坑，"今天想起来还很瘆人。"他说："我译这本书，与作者有共同的感受……"
>
> [The translator Gao Shan said, "The Chinese people, like the Jewish people, were ravaged in WWII ..." Gao told me [the journalist] that when he lived in Fuxin, Liaoning province, as a child, he saw with his own eyes the mass graves of the massacred Chinese laborers when the Japanese invaded China. "It's still unnerving to think about it today." He said, "I translated this book and had the same feelings with the author ... "] (Yuan 2010)

His own traumatic experience enables Gao to empathize with the primary witnesses' suffering and relay it to target readers. With the Japanese atrocities in his own memory, Gao believes he "had the same feelings with the author." This is where we get into the radical implications of the "translator as secondary witness" idea. If the translator is to try to recount the original author's story, better results can be achieved when that translator conveys it experientially. Representing the original Holocaust experience for his survivor authors is precisely the point of Gao's witnessing. To do that, the translated text has to possess an experiential "feel" for its recipients. Strictly speaking, of course, Gao cannot possibly convey the exact feeling of his authors' experiences because he did not go through the Holocaust himself. So if he wants to convey the lived experience of their trauma, he will need to generate this out of something else – specifically, out of that which most closely corresponds to the Holocaust in his own experience. Anything less would be to fail in his role as secondary witness. Gao reaches into his individual experience to find something comparable. This is why he turns to China's wartime encounter with Japanese atrocities.

Strictly speaking, however, the Holocaust is fundamentally different in several aspects from the Chinese wartime experience. David Engel discusses the Nazi notion of the "pathogen" essential to their drive to exterminate the Jews. While the Jews did not see themselves as essentially different from other people, they were singled out from their neighbors and considered "a pathogen that threatened to destroy all humanity" (Engel 2000, 4). For Hitler, the mission of eliminating the Jews was "a kind of crusade to redeem the world" (Friedländer 2008, xviii). Unlike the Jews, Chinese war victims knew they were part of an entire country under attack by foreign invaders. The Holocaust is also special in the way Nazis deliberately created what Primo Levi calls the "Lager," the camp and all it implied – a pitting of inmates against each other in a desperate struggle for survival. In this respect, the true horror of the "Lager" and by implication the Holocaust could come out: not just "us" against "them," (China vs Japan), but ultimately everyone against each other, (Jewish prisoners vs Jewish prisoners). Furthermore, the Holocaust was a highly systematic and sustained genocide. The Nazis made an industrial attempt to exterminate an entire people and culture from the world. They designed and perfected diabolically versatile systems of collective killing. They built gigantic death machines and deliberately, horrendously destroyed millions of human lives. The Japanese invaders did not. In the stationary, unchanging quality of prison conditions (vs dealing with an invading army passing through), or in terms of "playing for time" (hoping to defer execution long enough to merely survive), the Holocaust was clearly different.

To sum up, by drawing this analogy, Gao obviously smoothed out all these differences, and what disappears in the analogy is any sense of the distinctiveness of the Holocaust situation.

Whatever it lacks in rigor, the parallel appeared natural enough to Gao as he introduced Holocaust testimonies to his Chinese audience. The survivors' narrations jogged his own memory and he oscillated between personal experience and attuning to the originals' concentration camp world. In witnessing the Holocaust, he draws on the Japanese atrocities because they are the nearest equivalent to the European genocide for the receiving environment. They will pull the Chinese audience closer to the Jewish victims and thus enhance their empathetic engagement with Holocaust survivors. In this way, Gao contextualizes his translations by drawing a comparison not found in Western translations of Holocaust testimonies. His practice invites us to think about the *representability* of the Holocaust experience in an entirely different way. Specifically, it forces us to explore the extent to which *representability* (as the base for translation) is dependent on the experiential background of readers, and how an experience can be better represented, especially when there is no corresponding equivalent in the lived experience of its audience.

Rendering experiences a text wishes to convey can be a lot trickier than initially supposed; it isn't just a matter of conveying as accurately as possible the literal meaning of the original. Instead, the translator needs to consider how that text will work on its new audience, and the exact or specific effect it's likely to have on them. If the target audience for the translated text doesn't possess the same understanding of either the words or the phenomena described by the original, a literal translation is unlikely to be a success. If Chinese history includes nothing quite like the Nazi Lager, it can be extremely difficult for a Chinese audience to imagine such a place. Describing the closest experiential and cultural equivalent in introducing the Holocaust to China may be the best way to improve reception.

4.4 Secondary Witness in a Personal Way

Sharon Deane-Cox suggests that the role of secondary witness imposes ethical demands on the translator of Holocaust testimony, and she warns against drawing self-referential parallels, writing "this appropriative motion cannot and should not persist in the translation of traumatic memory" (2013, 312). "Any assimilation of the Holocaust victim's fractured selfhood to the translator's own recognizable and coherent markers will necessarily lead to the annihilation of the witness" (2013, 313). Primo Levi also calls attention to this problematic self-referential tendency, but he observes that it is "all the more difficult to avoid as the distance in space and time increases" (1989, 165). This is surely the case for Gao as the Holocaust happened far from China and nearly sixty years passed between the end of World War II and his translation work. Nonetheless, to render a particular Holocaust experience in China, it may be imperative for the translator to draw on something within the experience and cultural framework of the recipients.

Contrary to the objection to the translator's self-referential tendency, Gao uses his paratexts to assimilate the European Holocaust to the Chinese wartime experience. And while Deane-Cox insists that the translator "carry the ethical burden of guardianship" (2013, 321) to ensure the memory of survivors be accurately preserved and transmitted, Gao significantly alters the main texts of the testimonies according to his own standards of fluency and elegance, as analyzed in the previous section. In this respect, Gao takes his role as secondary witness in a highly personal way, attempting by radical means to make his witnessing as effective as possible.

There are actually scholars in Holocaust studies who promote a cosmopolitan idea of Holocaust memory, suggesting it can be expanded and lifted out of its European specificity, as long as "the uniqueness and exceptionalism attributed to its victim suffering for nationalist ends is abandoned and the field of memory is broadened to include other victims, other perpetrators and other bystanders involved in acts of mass violence and persecution" (Hirsch and Spitzer 2009, 165). The Holocaust, as an atrocity against humanity, has the power to evoke collective memories worldwide and transcend ethnic and national borders. Daniel Levy and Natan Sznaider also demonstrate an open-mindedness in proposing that "the Holocaust does not become one totalizing signifier containing the same meaning for everyone. Rather its meanings evolve from the encounter of global interpretations and local sensibilities" (Levy and Sznaider 2006, 11).

According to the research by Aaron Hass, at least one survivor, Ann Charnofsky, has emphasized that "people should remember not only my Holocaust, but other Holocausts" (Hass 1995, 194). The Japanese atrocities are the Chinese Holocaust. Even if some Western scholars consider the Holocaust unimaginable, inexpressible, and thus incomparable, for Gao, the Japanese invasion of China and the war crimes committed are also beyond words or imagination, and similar to the Holocaust in their brutality.

This inclination to assimilate and domesticate is rooted in the human mind and cannot be eradicated in practice. Peter Davies suggests that translators, through their translations, "contribute to, intervene in, and comment on ideas about the Holocaust at the specific moment when an act of witnessing crosses linguistic and cultural boundaries" (Davies 2018, 210). To understand and translate involves a hermeneutic process of procuring and appropriating. In this context, it becomes understandable that Gao presents a special perspective on the Holocaust which springs from the specific sociopolitical and historical circumstances of the recipient Chinese context.

5 Affect: The Translator's Stance in a Triangle Model

Holocaust testimony is a genre with highly affective potential. When survivors testify to their experience during the Holocaust, they are telling stories of a horrible period of human history when mass killings were severely inflicted on a particular group. To translate these stories is to reexperience the pain, wrath, shame, regret, guilt, and relief together with the authors. Affect, therefore, is a prominent and unsettling issue for the translation of Holocaust testimony.

In this section, I focus on the way Gao's translated texts function affectively. I found affect regarding not just the Jewish victims' suffering under Nazi persecution, but also parent–child relations inside the survivor's family, as well as Russian soldiers' crimes of robbery and rape in late-war Germany. To approach this, I resort to linguistic stance theories for a methodology. Stance is the expression of the internal mental state of a speaker, be it in spoken or written language. Stance-taking involves making an evaluative utterance that shows the speaker's knowledge, comment, and attitude toward the object being addressed. The model I chose is the stance triangle created by John W. Du Bois (2007) and modified by S. F. Kiesling and his colleagues (2018), with *affect* (or *evaluation*) as one of the three dimensions of stance analysis.

5.1 The Triangle of Stance

Scholars in sociolinguistics have studied stance in naturally occurring speaking and writing. In the view of Robert Englebretson, there are five key conceptual principles of stance which he summarizes as: "stance is physical/personal/moral, stance is public and interpretable, stance is interactional, stance is indexical, and stance is consequential" (Englebretson 2007, 11). First, stance consists in three overlapping levels: It is a physical act that involves body posture; it shows the attitude, belief, or evaluation of an individual person; and it is social morality that may involve moral judgment. The second principle holds that stance can be overtly inspected and interpreted in public. The third point refers to an inherent interactionality in stance, namely, stance as collaboratively constructed among many participants and relational to other stances. Fourth, stance calls up something beyond the textual and physical context and indexes the broader sociocultural background in which it occurs. Last but not

40 Translation and Interpreting

least, stance has consequences and leads to a real final result for the stancetaker. Englebretson believes that academic perspectives regarding stance tend to focus on any number of these five principles to varying degrees.

A common premise of many researches on stance in discourse lies in its heterogeneity. It is commonly recognized that stancetaking is an interactional practice by conversational co-participants, rather than an isolated action. As Elise Kärkkäinen asserts, "stances only emerge as a result of joint engagement in the evaluative activity" (2006, 712). And even if it looks like a personal stance, Alexandra Jaffe considers it "always achieved through comparison and contrast with other relevant persons and categories" (2009, 9). Participants in discourse do not evaluate an object in a vacuum; they do not merely act, they interact. Stance is a public action that is shaped by the voice and position of other stancetakers.

Taking this intersubjectivity into consideration, John W. Du Bois provides a basic structure for the representation of stance's components and their relations with each other. He first contextualizes stance in three questions: the identity of the stancetaker, the object of stance, and the prior stance being responded to. Then, he forges a unified framework for analyzing the realization and interpretation of stance (see Figure 3).

In this triangle, a single overarching, unified act of stance is explained with reference to three different aspects: evaluation, positioning, and alignment. There are two social actors represented in the triangle – the first and second subjects (the speakers who are making an evaluative utterance) – as well as the shared stance object (the entity being evaluated in those utterances). Stancetaking consists in three subsidiary acts of evaluating, positioning, and aligning. When Subject 1 signals an attitude or assessment toward the object, they are at the same time positioning themselves relative to the object, and this behavior is related, directed, and compared to how Subject 2 evaluates the same

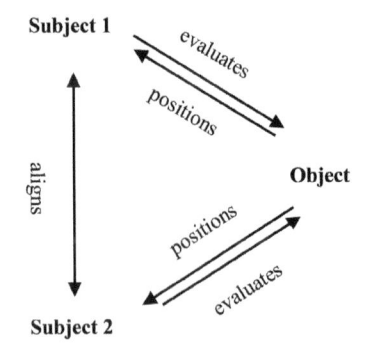

Figure 3 Du Bois's triangle of stance

object and situates themselves; alignment or disalignment can then be created from the similarity or difference of the two subjects' evaluations of the same object. As Du Bois summarizes: "Concomitant to evaluating a shared stance object, stancetakers position themselves. Concomitant to positioning themselves, stancetakers define alignment with each other, whether the alignment is convergent or divergent" (2007, 164). The concept of alignment as Du Bois uses it is nuanced, not black-or-white. Stance can be aligned or disaligned by subtle degrees. It represents a point along a continuous scale, rather than a binary choice between a positive vs a negative pole.

With Du Bois's stance triangle as a basis, Scott F. Kiesling and his colleagues have developed another model of stance. They modify one of the three aspects in Du Bois's stance triangle – evaluation – by noting how much the subject is invested in his evaluation, and then adding *investment* as one of the important dimensions of stance. In their definition, investment is essentially the strength or "holistic determination" (Kiesling et al. 2018, 686) of an utterance, which can be manifested by the extent to which the subject is willing to defend his claims and how epistemically certain they are. Therefore, to Kiesling, stance is a complex construct that is captured through three dimensions: affect, investment, and alignment. Affect refers to the language user's evaluation of the stance object, while investment denotes the degree to which that evaluation is felt. Alignment concerns how this user's evaluation relates to those of other users in the same dialogue. In a later review article in explaining the same model, Kiesling uses the old term *evaluation* (as a synonym of *affect*) and states clearly that the term refers to "the evaluation and positioning as outlined by Du Bois" (2022, 420). Thus, the term *affect* that Kiesling et al. employ is the combination of Du Bois's two dimensions, evaluation and positioning. Kiesling et al. also replace Du Bois's stance *object* with another term "stance focus," considering *focus* less reifying than *object*. Their new formulation can be seen in Figure 4 (and compared to Figure 3), though they did not draw their ideas into a triangle.

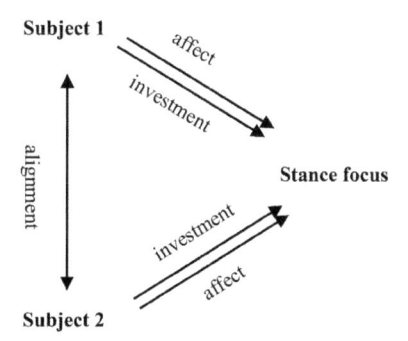

Figure 4 The stance triangle of Kiesling et al., adapted from Du Bois

To me, with their consideration of investment, Kiesling et al.'s new model presents a more comprehensive picture of the details of stancetaking than Du Bois's stance triangle. Moreover, their choice of the term "affect" is more pertinent to the topic I am addressing in this study. The survivor's affect plays a major role in Holocaust testimony as the personal and emotional bond between survivor and translator is often stressed. Thus, I will employ Kiesling's modified triangle with the three key aspects, *affect*, *investment*, and *alignment*, rather than Du Bois's *evaluation*, *positioning*, and *alignment*, to analyze Gao's translations. However, the ideas of both are based on an important quality inherent in the process of stancetaking – intersubjectivity. They both note that stance arises from the dialogic interaction between interlocutors in a conversational sequential context, and needs to be researched from an intersubjective vantage point.

Kiesling et al. use their triangle of stance in analyzing conversation threads from online forums. In a 2022 article, Robert Neather borrows the model for his study of online conversation about Buddhist translations. He focuses on discussion threads that debate the merits of published Buddhist translations on one online Buddhist forum, Dharma Wheel, and in particular translations of the *Lotus Sutra*. He studies the dialogues of several posts discussing and evaluating translations to examine how particular claims about translations are advanced in interaction, and how differences between participants are modulated or managed. Although Neather borrows Kiesling et al.'s model for his translation research, he actually applies it to online translation comment dialogues, the kind of texts these theories are made to be used on, rather than on translation itself.

Can the triangle of stance be applied to translations? One may question the feasibility of such an application by saying that the theoretical constructs all seem to be centered on interactions, made, in other words, to explicate interpersonal conversations, thus not suitable for analyzing actual translations. In order to apply stancetaking theories to translation, it is necessary to see translation as fundamentally dialogic or interactive. I here draw on the widely influential thought of dialogism, a theory that Mikhail Bakhtin adopts for interpreting language and the world. He suggests that meanings are always co-constructed, and that there is an interactional nature in every concrete utterance. Hence, the triangle of stance is applicable not just to straightforward, obviously conversational texts, but to all writings, including translation.

5.2 Bakhtin and Dialogism

Dialogism, a lifelong focus of Bakhtin's theoretical quest, lent itself readily to novels, which he viewed as primordially dialogical. Instead of treating a work as hermetic and self-sufficient, Bakhtin imagines it "a rejoinder in a given dialogue, whose style is determined by its interrelationship with other rejoinders in the same dialogue ... " (1996, 274) And the living utterances "arise out of this dialogue as a continuation of it and as a rejoinder to it ... " (1996, 276–277) Novels, in his view, embody a dynamic interplay and interruption of different perspectives represented by various characters. Their distinct voices speak for themselves in their own reality, subverting the author's monopoly of the text.

To Bakhtin, dialogism is essential not only in literary texts but in language generally. Dialogue is a pervasive force in language, because a single consciousness is always addressing an intense relationship with others and there is always a "dialogic orientation of a word among other words (of all kinds and degrees of otherness)" (Bakhtin 1996, 275). "Language ... lies on the borderline between oneself and the other. The word in language is half someone else's" (Bakhtin 1996, 293). Bakhtin even deconstructs the concept of monologue, considering it an illusory, relative construct necessarily made to understand dialogue. If it shows physically as a monologue, it is essentially a dialogue. Within this mindset, thoughts can be deemed inner dialogue, so there are already dialogues existing in the speaking subject's mental event before an utterance is possible.

Bakhtin insists that verbal discourse has a social soul, and is not self-contained. The use of language is mediated by social ways of seeing, which always illuminate some aspects of an object and obscures others, and which are always challenged and changed in dialogues (Robinson 2011). Bakhtin finds the speaking subject never an isolated entity:

> ... every actually spoken word (or comprehensibly written one) ... is an expression and product of the social interaction of three components: –the speaker (author), the listener (reader), and the one of whom (or of which) they speak (the hero). The word is a social event, it is not sufficient in itself ... A concrete utterance (and not a linguistic abstraction) is born, lives and dies in the process of the social interaction of the participants in the utterance. (Voloshinov and Bakhtin[12] 1983, 17)

Language is the medium ground of individual and group relations, and it is the dialogicality of language that absorbs individuals into groups while enabling them to remain themselves (Holquist 1990, 57). Utterances are achieved under preexisting restraints, being conditioned by prior utterances, particular group practices and social norms. Every utterance is made as a response to something and may expect responses in turn, and they are constantly in conversation with each other. Therefore, the authentic environment in which an utterance lives and

---

[12] The source of this quote is the essay titled "Discourse in life and discourse in poetry," and may or may not be written by Bakhtin. It could be by V. N. Voloshinov.

takes shape is dialogized heteroglossia. A person is always in dialogue with something in the world. Their verbal discourse has to relate to the extraverbal situation that engenders it.

Bakhtin's idea of dialogism endows every verbal utterance with a quality of interactivity, and lays the theoretical foundation for viewing translation from an intersubjective perspective. A translated text can be a dialogical whole. The translator may convey evaluations explicitly or implicitly in response to the evaluations made by other subjects, thus making the translated text an intense, complicated arena with various forces of different discourse co-participants. Translation embodies multiple voices and conveys meanings beyond the literal words on the page. Some scholars of translation studies have pointed out the multiple, even mutually contradictory, voices in translation, which are actually forms of stance-taking. Theo Hermans focuses on the translators' position, a concept similar to stance, and proposes that "all translating can be seen to have the translator's subject position inscribed in it" (Hermans 2014a, 286). "The translator both speaks for the original author and signals reservations" (Hermans 2014b, 65). By drawing on Relevance Theory, Hermans views translation as an instance of "echoic speech," suggesting that the translator may indicate an opinion regarding his translation which can be empathetic and supportive, or skeptical and dissociative. And in the latter case, the echoic speech becomes an ironic speech, meaning that the translator is implying a distancing and disapproving attitude. When translators voice their attitudes, they are taking a stance in the translation activity.

5.3 Gao's Stance in a Triangle Model

Kiesling et al.'s triangle of stance can be used to examine Gao's stance-taking when he intervenes into the original texts and inserts additions of his own devising. Specifically, I will analyze Gao's affects toward the suffering of the Jews under Nazi rule, the authors' family life, and the misconduct of Russian soldiers, and note the intensity of those affects and how they align or disalign with the affects toward the same object held by the authors and the Chinese publisher. My objective is to explore how Gao mediates his affects and positions himself in relation to the authors and the publisher.

5.3.1 Jewish Victims' Suffering

In writing their stories, both Max Stern and Olga Horak describe the hardships they endured under Nazi rule, including the pain of wandering about in desperation under endless apprehension, the horror of witnessing innumerable murders, long struggles with nightmares, and nervous breakdowns. Comparison of the original text with its translation reveals Gao's inclination to intensify the authors' description of these sufferings.

One example is Stern's description of his worst camp experience in Sachsenhausen. He narrates how, upon arrival, the prisoners were shaved, numbered, and told to assemble for inspection, and how a priest was shot by a commandant right on the spot. Stern's narration is flat, without color or emotion. Gao appears to think it would not sufficiently attract reader's attention, so he added the following remarks to Stern's narration:

> 这里只有屠杀和血腥，没有人性，没有尊严。那些持枪的人都是野兽，可以不眨眼地屠杀一位母亲、儿童和老人。
>
> [There was nothing but carnage and bloodshed, no humanity, no dignity. The men with guns were monsters who could kill a mother, child, or elderly person without blinking an eye.] (Stern 2004, 48)

This addition gives a more direct insight into the horror of the concentration camps. It was quoted by the journalist Yuan Xi in the news report reviewing the book in *People's Daily* on January 9, 2005. Yuan may not have known it stemmed from Gao, instead of the author's original text, but he clearly considered these words precise and effective to introduce the situation of the Nazi camp to the Chinese audience.

Another example concerns Olga Horak's experience at Kurzbach, a subcamp of Gross-Rosen concentration camp in Germany. In late 1944, Horak and her mother were transported from Auschwitz-Birkenau to Kurzbach, where they spent the harsh winter of 1944–1945. She describes the life there, including the prisoners' housing in a barn with bunks, the camp's exposed latrines, the endless roll calls, prisoners' slave labor in the forest, and other daily routines. There were two female SS guards, who acted no less viciously than their male colleagues. They carried canes for beating the prisoners whenever they wanted:

> **Original:**
> They were dressed in the uniform of the female SS, a field grey outfit with a heavy warm cape and the ever-present cane for striking prisoners. (Horak 2000, 53)
>
> **Translation:**
> 她们穿着女式的党卫军军服，一件灰色的带有斗篷的衣服，手里拿着棍棒，不时地毒打囚犯。很多囚犯被毒打得急剧地抽搐，无力尖叫，只能痛苦地呻吟。听到她们的嚎叫，许多囚犯不由自主地哆嗦起来。
>
> [They were dressed in the uniform of the female SS, a grey outfit with cape, and held canes in their hands striking prisoners savagely every now and then. Many of the prisoners were so badly beaten that they twitched severely, unable to scream, and could only moan in pain. Hearing their howls, many of the prisoners shivered involuntarily.] (Horak 2010, 60)

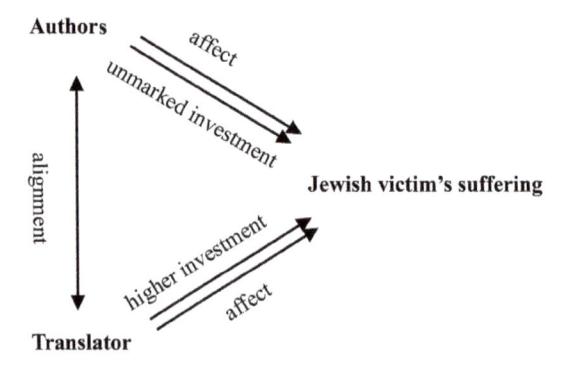

Figure 5 The translator's stance vis-à-vis Jewish victim's suffering

To the original's mere statement of the act of beating, Gao supplies the image of prisoners desperately struggling under violent physical assaults, as it is underlined. Through picturing this, the target readers will more deeply feel the terror and despair of the Jewish prisoners. Such additions indicate the stance Gao takes regarding the Jewish victims' suffering, which is clear when I present it in the form of a triangle. As a person with a sense of justice and compassion, Gao closely accords with his authors, but he amplifies the original narratives by increasing their intensity and volume, thus investing more heavily in portraying the suffering of Jewish victims. Figure 5 shows his relation with the authors in evaluating their and their fellow prisoners' suffering.

When translating trauma, Gao attains emotional resonance through visualizing the original words. He has so immersed himself into the camp world that he cannot help but weave some of his own thoughts and imagination into the narrative. His personal connection with his good friend Stern and with Horak naturally makes him keen to bear witness for them. Thinking himself sharing their feelings, he is eager to speak out for the friends he treasures, and is determined to amplify the voices of the weak and defend the oppressed against Nazi injustice, from a position of righteous indignation.

5.3.2 The Authors' Family Life

Gao also makes evaluative utterances on the authors' family life by altering and enriching the originals. A radical example concerns a minor conflict between the teenage Horak and her mother. In 1942–1943, Horak's family was hiding in Hungary. As the adults were struggling with anxiety in the face of imminent danger, tempers briefly flared. The underlined is where Gao's translation differs from the original:

Original:
… one day my mother was very upset, and I was the one who <u>copped it</u>. (Horak 2000, 18)

Translation:
有一天, 母亲十分不高兴, <u>是我惹的祸。</u>

[One day, my mother was very upset, and I was the one who <u>caused the problem.</u>] (Horak 2010, 23)

When Horak writes "copped," she means her mother was venting her anger, unfairly, on her daughter. But Gao lays the blame on Horak, criticizing her for causing her mother's upset. When Horak talks back to her mother, the mother overreacts and hits her. The original text ends the episode by saying that Horak never forgot being hit by her mother on that occasion, and that she felt deeply hurt and refused to talk to anybody for days. But Gao was clearly not happy with it. He made the following additions to the original:

于是我终于向母亲道出了心思, 请求母亲原谅。令我欣慰的是, 她的反应非常平静。"我的孩子, "她对我说, "妈妈早忘了。"母亲的这番话使我如释重负。从那以后, 我们母女俩的心贴得更近了。

[I finally told my mother what was in my mind and asked for her forgiveness. To my relief, her reaction was very calm. "My child," she said to me, "I've already forgotten about it." Mother's words freed me from a grievous burden. Since then, our hearts have been closer.] (Horak 2010, 23)

Gao adds this because the original ending does not conform to the key Chinese philosophical concept of "filial piety," or *xiao*, so cherished in Chinese society. "Filial piety" is a Confucian virtue which advocates the child's obedience, respect, duty, and caring for the parents. James St. André has traced the historical development of the English term filial piety and its conflation with *xiao*, suggesting that this attribute has a long tradition in China and today is seen as mainly specific to China (2018, 310). In accordance with this virtue, Gao made Horak examine herself and apologize to her mother, because a properly pious girl is more likely to leave a favorable impression on the target readers compared to a heartless child who bears grudges against her parent.

The passage reveals a tension of evaluative attitudes toward parent–child relations between the translator and the author, which can be shown in Figure 6. The tone in which Horak talks about the conflict is quite realistic. She feels aggrieved at being wronged by her mother and registers a bitter complaint about her mother's overreaction. Her investment does not receive

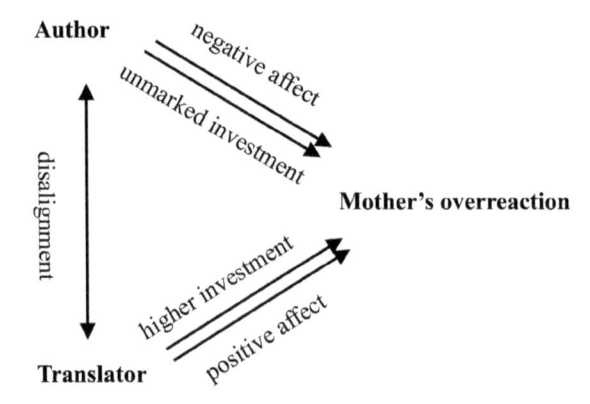

Figure 6 The translator's stance vis-à-vis parent–child relation

any particular emphasis but Gao intensifies this investment by altering and adding to the original text, making Horak admit to "her" mistake and ask for forgiveness. In drawing on the conventional Chinese virtue of filial piety and reframing the scene, Gao is, to an extent, disaligning himself with his author. As he imbues the scene with values absent in (though not necessarily incompatible with) the original, he takes a certain divergent stance relative to that of the author.

In order to enhance the target readers' acceptance of the author's life story, Gao elaborates various scenes, creating a well-rounded picture in line with his own vision of how, in an ideal world, family relations might develop. In the opening paragraph of *Auschwitz to Australia*, while Horak simply introduces her home city and family members, Gao added numerous details to render it a harmonious environment with exemplary parenting. When translating Max Stern's book, Gao gives an idealistic touch to the love relationship between Stern and his wife Eva, and emphasizes Stern's marital loyalty.

By idealizing the family life depicted in the originals into a morality model, Gao is appealing to the values he shares with the target society. The concept of family in Chinese culture expresses the idea of collective harmony and is deeply rooted in the Chinese social order. The traditional family mindset is "an integrated part of the Chinese welfare ideology" (Hämäläinen et al. 2017, 234). Individuals, with clear and determined roles within the family, contribute to a harmonious social life. In this light, Gao adapted the authors' families to the way of Chinese welfare thinking, playing to stereotypical social expectations in the target context.

5.3.3 Russian Soldiers' Misdeeds

Both Stern and Horak describe in their books how, toward the end of the war, when the Soviet Red Army entered Germany, robberies and rape of German women were regular occurrences. However, this information is carefully changed or removed in Gao's translations. In May 1945, Stern and other prisoners from the Sachsenhausen concentration camp were liberated during their death march. Shortly after they were treated in a Russian field hospital, they set out on their journey home. When they reached Spandau, the main headquarters of the Russian army in Germany, they saw two Russian soldiers standing at the entrance with machine guns. This is what happened:

> **Original:**
> A German woman came up to them and <u>complained she had been raped.</u> One soldier replied in Yiddish: "<u>What should I do?</u> Go home, go home." (Stern 2003, 68)
>
> **Translation:**
> 一个德国妇女走上前，向他们投诉，一个士兵用依地语回答："我没有办法，回家吧，回家吧。"
>
> [A German woman came up to them and <u>complained.</u> A soldier replied in Yiddish: "<u>I can do nothing.</u> Go home, go home."] (Stern 2004, 58)

The translation differs from the original text in two places, where underlined. The woman's specific complaint – the rape – is omitted, in favor of the Russian image. Furthermore, in the original, the soldier answers the woman with a rhetorical question "What should I do?" implying his indifference and coldness, which is changed into a less negative, declarative "I can do nothing." An odd detail is that the soldier answers in Yiddish, a language spoken by Jews in Eastern Europe, including in parts of Russia. He therefore must have been Jewish and understood what the woman said in German. In a similar case, when Stern mentions that shortly after the war, civilians traveling on trains were frequently robbed by Russian soldiers, the translation refrains from mentioning that it was the Russians who committed these robberies.

In the translation of Olga Horak's book, we find a more radical move to avoid casting the Russians in a negative light. The example concerns the "short walk" a Russian officer took with Horak's friend Bozena. After liberation from the camps, Horak was sent to a hospital where she met another young female patient called Bozena; they quickly became very good friends. One day, as they were sitting in a park, a Russian officer stopped to talk with Bozena. To their surprise, the officer wore ten watches on his arm, and Bozena boldly asked him to give her one of his watches. The officer said yes but what he asked in return seems to make Gao uncomfortable and the story is changed:

Original:
"Yes," he said, "Charasho—why not. But come with me for a short walk first." Bozena left the park bench and went for the "short walk" with the Russian officer. I had no idea where they went, but when she returned an hour later, she showed me a beautiful gold bracelet watch which the Russian had given her. No questions were asked. (Horak 2000, 92)

Translation:
"好",军官说,"没问题,为什么不可以呢?但你要先陪我出去见我一个朋友。我在和他打赌,赌在一个小时内就能找到一位女朋友,你就装扮成我的女友。"波兹娜爽快地从长椅上站了起来, 陪苏军军官去见他的朋友。我也不知道他们去了哪里, 功夫不大她就回来了。她让我看了苏军军官给她的一块漂亮的金表,那是她假扮军官女友得到的礼物。

["Yes", said the officer, "why not? But first you have to go out with me to meet a friend of mine. I'm making a bet with him that I'll find a girlfriend within an hour and you'll pretend to be my girlfriend." Bozena got up from the bench readily and accompanied the Russian officer to meet his friend. I had no idea where they went, but she came back after a short time. She showed me a beautiful gold watch that the Soviet officer had given her, as a gift for acting as his girlfriend.] (Horak 2010, 100)

Clearly, Bozena had sex with the Russian officer to obtain that watch. But the translation offers an altogether more innocent, light-hearted story that depicts the Russian as friendly and generous. What is behind such changes? Commenting on the translation of *The Max Factor* (accessed on September 10, 2022), Gao said he once approached Stern to check the incidents involving Russian misconduct. Stern assured him that the robberies and rapes were accurately depicted. Gao himself had a bit of relevant experience as well: When living in north-eastern China in his early years, he was often told by older residents that when the Soviet Red Army marched into Manchuria to destroy the Japanese Kwantung Army,[13] robberies and rapes were common in their land. One might then have expected him to adhere to the truth and maintain the relevant passages fully intact in his translation. However, he suggested that he was challenged by the Chinese publisher, who exerted strong pressure on him to downplay this content, stating that the translation could not be published otherwise.

---

[13] In August 1945, the Soviet Union poured its soldiers into Japanese-occupied Manchuria in northeastern China to defeat the Kwantung Army of Japan. This military operation was significant in accelerating Japan's surrender and bring hostilities of the war in East Asia to a close.

Gao's claim can't be verified. But I do not have reason to doubt his words. It seems that the publisher may well have imposed such a pressure in the political context of China–Russia relations at that time.

After the end of the Cold War, China and Russia established various bilateral and multilateral cooperation mechanisms out of a common desire to offset the hegemonic position of the United States and create a multipolar international system. During the 1990s and early 2000s, the two countries intensified their good relationship, developed close ties with each other, and became increasingly united by largely convergent views of international issues. In April 1996, China and Russia established the Shanghai Five (a group of five countries: China, Russia, Kazakhstan, Kyrgyzstan, and Tajikistan), which upgraded to the Shanghai Cooperation Organization in June 2001 with deeper political and economic connections. In July of the same year, the two sides signed the Treaty on Good Neighborliness, Friendship, and Cooperation; China has no such friendship treaty with any other country (Bekkevold 2022, 47). The two forged a "strategic partnership" and resolved that their friendship "would pass down for all generations" (Wilson 2004, 3). When Russian President Vladimir Putin visited China in October 2004 and signed an agreement to resolve decades-long border disputes, the strategic trust between the two sides further deepened.

China and Russia's societal links also grew significantly from the mid-2000s (Li and Poh 2019, 28). The Sino-Russian People-to-People Cooperation Council organized various social events to increase cultural exchanges between the two countries. For example, 2006 was "the Year of Russia" in China and 2007 "the Year of China" in Russia; "the Chinese Language Year" and "the Russian Language Year" were also held in 2009–2010. In other words, the very years Gao was working on the translations and pursuing their publication saw a rapid consolidation of Sino-Russian partnership. In this process, China was active in initiating and pursuing the partnership, and the Chinese leadership often showing a highly solicitous attitude in seeking good relations with Russia. The Posts and Telecom Press, as a state-owned publishing enterprise, obviously followed the course set by the government. This correlates with their unwillingness to publish material containing negative depictions of the Russian.

The examples display Gao's evaluative attitudes in a complicated tension. In the stance triangle shown as Figure 7, I add colors to the different properties of attitudes. Both Stern and Horak hold negative affect (red) toward Russian misdeeds, with definite, high investment. But the publisher holds a positive affect (green) toward them and puts strong pressure on the translator. The translator personally feels inclined to stand with the authors (green) and disagrees with the publisher (red), but in an attempt to align himself with the

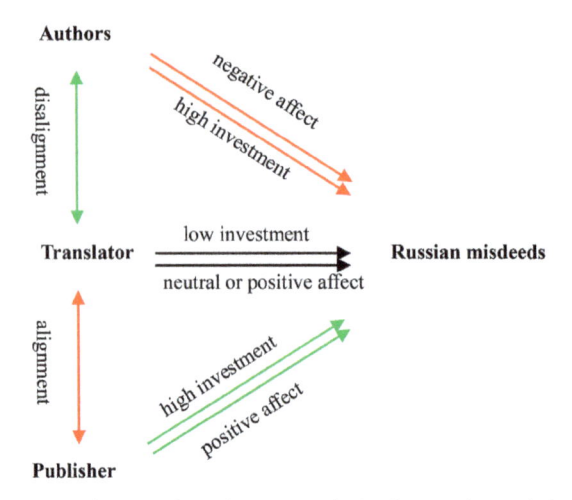

Figure 7 The translator's stance vis-à-vis Russian misdeeds

publisher's politics, he feels obliged to reduce the investment in truthfully reporting Russian misdeeds and avoid showing a negative affect toward them. The mixture of different colors shows the dilemma the translator faced. Gao is squeezed in the middle of a tension: He wants to witness for the authors, but he is also under pressure from the publisher.

Kiesling et al.'s triangle model, though originally used to analyze the stance of speakers in conversational exchange, proves equally useful in discerning the translator's positioning relative to that of other participants in translated texts. Gao performs an affective intervention into the original texts, whether from his own volition or under pressure from the publisher. He intensifies the description of the Jewish victims' suffering out of eagerness to witness for his survivor friends; he projects stereotypical Chinese social expectations on the authors' family life to create scenes familiar to prospective readers; and he redescribes the misdeeds by some Russian soldiers with a light touch so as to form a reluctant alignment with his publisher in a Russia-friendly political environment. This brings up what we see in the finished translations: stronger accusations of the Nazis' atrocities, idealized love among family members, and deliberate obliteration of the Russian soldiers' crimes due to politically motivated lenience.

Conclusion: Out of the Ordinary

The survivor authors are the chroniclers and memorialists of one of the darkest epochs in human history. Their testimonies constitute crucial and invaluable documents of the Holocaust at the individual level. Many of the survivors are repeatedly pulled back into the overwhelming fear and sorrow, but this does not mean they live in the past. It is the past that lives in them. Notwithstanding the passage of time, their testimonies carry within them the indelible memory of the dead and a startling warning from history. Translation is an indispensable means of disseminating this memory and warning. If Holocaust memories are to transcend linguistic boundaries, translation plays a vital role in their migration, mutation, and maintenance, keeping them alive in many foreign territories.

Despite the fact that Holocaust testimonies have been translated into Chinese for over half a century, the impact of translation on their republication and retransmission in China has gone largely uncharted. My project explores the journey taken by two works of Holocaust testimony originally written in English, one by Max Stern and the other by Olga Horak, from their original publication in Australia to their Chinese translation. Through contextualization and comparison of the translated texts with the originals, I analyze how the translator Gao Shan plays a transformative role in adjusting the two authors' Holocaust experience to a prospective Chinese audience.

I began this study with an account of the lives of the two authors and the translator. Gao established a close personal connection with Max Stern in the commercial field of the international stamp trade. Deeply touched by Stern's stories of the Holocaust, Gao translated Stern's and then Stern's cousin Olga Horak's memoirs into Chinese. Though not a professional translator, he drew on Yan Fu's time-honored principles of translation (*xin, da,* and *ya*: fidelity, readability, and elegance) and decided to focus on enhancing readability and elegance, as shown in my analysis of Gao's poetics of translation and how it is reflected in the actual translations.

I marshaled concepts from sociology, memory studies, and sociolinguistics to gain a handle on the specific features of Gao's translations. Pierre Bourdieu's concept of habitus proved helpful in elucidating Gao's liberal translation practice as he transferred his professional disposition as a well-placed company official to his work as a translator. His prominence in the postal field affords him considerable autonomy in producing his translation, without being strictly constrained by the original texts.

The role of a secondary witness helps to justify Gao's clear subject position when translating and to elucidate his way of presenting the translations to target readers. It enlightened our understanding not only of his insistence on showing the personal bond between himself and his authors but also his juxtaposition of the European Holocaust with Japanese military crimes committed in China. Gao's inclination to reference the wartime experience springing from the recipient Chinese historical context, and his substantial alterations to the main texts of the testimonies to align with his standards of fluency and elegance, demonstrate his dedication to engaging in secondary witnessing in a deeply personal manner.

The triangle of stance with three dimensions, *affect*, *investment*, and *alignment*, provided a methodology to examine the evaluative attitude Gao signals in his translations regarding Jewish victims' suffering, the survivors' family life, and the wrongdoings of Russian soldiers. Even though the model was originally developed for analyzing the stance of speaking subjects in conversational exchanges, it proved effective in illustrating how Gao mediates his affect and positions himself relative to the authors and the Chinese publisher in his translated testimonies. We saw him intensifying the authors' description of Holocaust victims' suffering, playing to stereotypical values of family life embedded in the target culture, and having to bow to pressure from the publisher to avoid any negative portrayal of the Russian military.

The liberties Gao takes make his translations extremely unusual in the context of Holocaust testimony translation. Some authors of Holocaust testimony, like Primo Levi, demand of their translator's absolute fidelity to the original text. Levi was not only a chemist, writer, and Holocaust survivor, but also a practitioner and theorist of translation. His translingual experience in camps makes translation a "remarkable persistence" throughout his work and "a defining feature of his writing" (Alexander 2007, 167). In *The Drowned and the Saved*, Levi elaborated on translation issues with the German translator of his memoir *If This Is a Man*. He asked for the draft of the translation to be sent to him in batches, and checked "not merely its lexical but also its inner faithfulness" (Levi 1989, 170). "Driven by a scruple of superrealism" (Levi 1989, 172), he was obsessed with accuracy and word-for-word fidelity. He wanted nothing lost of his Italian original in its German garment, demanding from his translator a reproduction of the original text, more a tape recording than a book. Some scholars also propose ethical strictness in translating Holocaust testimony. Sharon Deane-Cox wanted the translator to listen to the original traumatic narratives perceptively and accomplish as accurately as possible a reconstruction of the original testimony in every detail that "preserves and perpetuates the contours of the survivor's memory" (2013, 322).

When Levi and Deane-Cox first expressed their demand for absolute fidelity in translation, their concern was that nothing should be omitted of the horror, the unspeakability, and of the original Holocaust experience. Their anxiety or worry was that by altering the text translators might thereby fail to convey the full extremity of what was actually experienced. However, Gao didn't hesitate to add material about stamps to the authors' Holocaust memories in order to secure publication of their testimony, while freely omitting textual details he considered unimportant, as well as adding and rearranging certain descriptions according to his own taste. Clearly, there's no way we can pretend his translations don't differ – and in some ways even radically – from their original sources. And through trying to draw an analogy between the Holocaust and Chinese wartime experiences, he is only exacerbating those differences. Hence, Gao's translations provoke serious ethical concerns.

The ethics of the translator of Holocaust lives has garnered academic attention. Peter Davies addresses this issue by comparing the very different research approaches of Holocaust Studies and Translation Studies. He points out that scholars in Holocaust studies are usually preoccupied with the victim-witnesses, their first-hand experiences, and the verbal accounts of these experiences. Researchers who proceed from this thinking in Holocaust studies and view the translator as secondary witness, are apt to place the voice of the victim above all other factors and demand absolute faithfulness to the original texts. However, translation studies have long shifted from discussions of fidelity and textual equivalence to a much more complex series of concerns including translator as an active agent and potential effects of target culture. Translation scholars see translation as a subjective activity that, while not based on a fixed set of rigorous rules, always involves the translators' appreciating, thinking, and judging minds. Lawrence Venuti intentionally produces highly heterogeneous translations to advocate for the translator's autonomy. When translating the nineteenth-century Italian novel *Fosca,* Venuti employed extensive archaism to signal its historical origin, British spellings to enhance its strangeness for American readers, and jarring lexical combinations to remind readers they are engaging with a translation. In this way, he seeks to undermine some of the illusions readers tend to project onto translated works, including the naive assumption that his translation offers a perfect equivalent to the original text. For him, translation "depends fundamentally on the translator's interpretation of the foreign text" (Venuti 1998, 16). Here, those who study Holocaust testimony translation have unanimously recognized the crux of the problem: "The need of survivors to be assured that the translation is an authentic and transparent rendering of their words clashes with the discoveries of Translation Studies scholars that question not only this possibility, but also its desirability" (Boase-Beier et al. 2017, 6). Gao's translations, with the liberties he takes, escalate this divergence.

Peter Davies considers it unrealistic to demand that translation of Holocaust testimony mirror the original exactly. If in theory translators are expected to transfer every minute aspect of the original and are forbidden to feed their own ideas, beliefs, knowledge, or attitudes into a text, in practice "only a tiny minority might go some way toward fulfilling the demands of a theory like this" (Davies 2018, 15). On the whole, I agree with Peter Davies's critique of the demand for literal faithfulness. Indeed, Gao in his treatment went far beyond the normal scope of a translator's duties. Apart from tailoring his portrayal of Russian soldiers to a special political context, the extent to which he privileged fluency and elegance over fidelity, intensified the description of Jewish victims' suffering and reshaped the authors' family life are all obviously extravagant. He made obtrusive alterations to the original to conform to the notions and prejudices of a given public. Clearly, Gao's translation practice doesn't fit the mold set up by Levi. However, it seems to me that Levi's demands of textual accuracy are perhaps ultimately too stringent to be practical. His relentless pursuit of total, absolute fidelity to the original renders translation a superhuman task.

In fact, Levi himself translated in a way very different from what he professed. In his essay "On Translating and Being Translated," Levi posited a linguistic sensitivity as necessary, enabling a translator to identify with the author and detect the original's shortcomings which (according to Levi) may be the fault of the author but pose some invisible pitfalls for the translator (Levi 2003). However, as Lina N. Insana noted, what Levi didn't make explicit in the essay was that as a translator he actually "felt compelled to correct those gaps and missteps in the service of goals that reached beyond the source text and into his own aesthetic, moral, and ethical world view" (Insana 2009, 228). Insana's study of Levi's translation of Franz Kafka's *Der Prozeß* (*The Trial*) as an ur-Holocaust work foreshadowing Auschwitz reveals a paradoxically interventionist approach in which Levi puts himself in the position of outright contention with the original: He smoothed out Kafka's writing style, replaced the original's incompleteness and ambiguities with a veneer of unproblematic integrity, and shifted the linguistic focus to reflect his own concerns and understanding of the protagonist (Insana 2009, 224–225).[14] Despite his claim of attempting fidelity to the original, his specific domesticating strategies and decision to obscure instances of his own mediation result in a text "as much Levi's own as Kafka's" (Insana 2009,186).

For Levi, then, translating and being translated appear to involve distinctly different requirements. He described how, when caught up in the taxing experience of being translated, one becomes afraid of "seeing one's thoughts manhandled, refracted, one's painstakingly chosen word transformed or misunderstood, or even invigorated by some unhoped for resource in the host

---

[14] Though a debated issue, many scholars have long recognized Kafka's foreshadowing of the Nazi Holocaust. For example, Theodor W. Adorno discusses the proximity of Kafka's world to that of the Third Reich, suggesting that Kafka's prophecy of terror and torture was realized in fascism (1967, 259–260). George Steiner views Kafka as uncovering the inner roots of Nazism, his nightmare vision containing forebodings of the horror gathering, the death factories, and the later catastrophe. *The Trial*, as Steiner considers it, "exhibits the classic model of the terror state" (1976, 121). Sidra Ezrahi also notes that Auschwitz appears nearly as the realization of the fantastical world depicted in Kafka's fiction (1980, 5). Hence, there is nothing inappropriate to reading *The Trial* as an ur-Holocaust text.

language" (Levi 1989, 172). That explains his notorious concern with literal accuracy in the translation of his works. He meticulously reviewed the renditions of his texts to ensure there was no deviation from his original intent, demanding that the interlingual transference involved take place transparently, without any trace of translational artifacts. However, Insana has found that "in his own translation work, despite frequent recourse to a rhetoric of transparency and identification ... Levi's tendency was towards a certain translatorly intervention" (Insana 2009, 183). His transformation of the source text for his own purposes clearly reflects a desire to exert control over the meaning of the Holocaust. This double standard implies that the actual practice of translation can deviate from the ethical demands imposed on translators. While high ethical standards can be articulated in theory, their implementation in translation practice may vary significantly.

Due to the intricacies in practice, many translations of Holocaust testimonies cannot be identical to their originals. Perhaps a typical example is Elie Wiesel's production of the French work entitled *La Nuit* [The Night] (1958) in the 1950s from compressing, reshaping, and thoroughly gallicizing his Yiddish original testimony *Un die Velt hot geschwign* [And the world remained silent] (1956). David Bellos has pointed out that, for the first forty years of *La Nuit*'s existence, only a few Jewish scholars knew this work was actually a translation (2022, 15). And a translation that had undergone significant alterations from the original: According to Naomi Seidman's examination, the Jewish rage in the Yiddish original disappears in the French version. So while the Yiddish version depicts how some liberated Jewish boys ran off to steal provisions and rape German girls by way of revenge against the Germans, the French version has them merely going off to look for clothes and sex, with no sign of any other motive. Clearly, a "scene of lawless retribution" by the survivors was altered to "a far more innocent picture" (Seidman 1996, 6). At the end of the Yiddish original, Wiesel shows himself alive with eagerness for vengeance and fury at the world's indifference and forgetting – all of which was suppressed in the French version by foregrounding a reticent and mournful Jew. As David Roskies observes, while the Yiddish original concludes with Wiesel's appeal to oppose Germans and anti-Semites seeking to consign the Holocaust to oblivion, the French version merely voices existential despair. By way of explanation Roskies offers that "since no one in the literary establishment of the 1950s was ready to be preached to by a Holocaust survivor, existential doubt became the better part of valor" (Roskies 1984, 301). Decidedly, these substantial changes in translation indicate a deliberate attempt to ingratiate the author with a non-Jewish world. So while Wiesel had to put up with a good deal of criticism for misrepresenting his original Yiddish Holocaust experience, his

French translation was disseminated successfully and became "the first to reach a worldwide audience in a whole series of subsequent translations" (Bellos 2022, 15).

Likewise, Gao encountered his own specific circumstances while translating the testimonies of the two authors. Geographical distance from Europe and the absence of a significant Jewish survivor population have limited China's engagement with the Western tradition of Holocaust testimony in books, films, documentaries, and other media. Many Chinese readers, while appreciating the famous diary of Anne Frank, might not be sufficiently intrigued by a book written by an ordinary Jew detailing his personal experience of the Holocaust, particularly if the writing style is seen as rough and unrefined. We have to remember that Gao's translations arose not from any preexisting interest in the subject, either in himself or his imagined Chinese readers – he was accepting a request from a Jewish friend due to their personal bond. So Gao, in effect, felt he had to *create* an audience for Horak's and Stern's memoirs in China. He serves as a communicator who passes on survivors' Holocaust experiences rather than that of a mechanical replicator who (as some Holocaust scholars would have it) simply presents a replication of a text.

Consequently, for Gao to bring these testimonies to life in China, ensuring that his friends, as Holocaust survivors, would be heard took precedence over concerns with linguistic accuracy. His first priority was to get ordinary Chinese readers to see and understand what had happened, and if some details got in the way, he felt free to decide how to handle them. He translates out of an impulse to help the testimonies cross linguistic boundaries and live in a new cultural environment. This led to his adopting nonstandard translation practices. To draw attention to the authors' personal history of the Holocaust, he had to connect it, in his paratexts, to the Chinese wartime experience and intervene in the original text, so that his translation would resonate with an audience for whom it was all still so new.

Gao's translations help to illuminate an issue previously avoided in Holocaust testimony scholarship: the unavoidability of changes in translation, based on the cultural environment of the target audience. Since every social space is already culturally colored, translation is never transmission to a neutral area. Due to vast internal and external complexities in the recipient context, translators are always entangled in a web of personal, cultural and historical forces, and many translated texts, in reality, cannot hope to achieve complete fidelity to the original. As a result, the translation of Holocaust testimony can never be a matter of simple transparency. It involves complicated relations between text and context, with at least some changes being unavoidable due to the need to adapt a text for a new readership. In his monograph *Witness Between Languages*, Peter Davies studies the translations of a range of Holocaust testimonies, adopting a target-audience perspective so as to expose comparative awareness in considering variations between translations. He argues that the different contexts in which these texts are placed require the use of different cultural references in the narratives, and he provides plenty of examples illustrating how the translator's addition or deletion of cultural information and changes of emphasis in the translated texts cater to the target circumstances (Davies 2018).

We might think of all this in terms of an analogy. According to Einstein's theory of general relativity, light rays (contrary to what we suppose) actually bend in going around the sun. Likewise, at first glance, the fidelity of a translation to its original text would appear to call for something like straight linear movement (word-for-word fidelity). But in practice it doesn't work that way. Instead, because of the gravitational pull of circumstances, any translation hoping for comprehension within a particular cultural context will have to "bend" to suit the circumstances of that context.

Translating Holocaust testimony is never merely a matter of mechanical, one-size-fits-all linguistic replication. Any view of translation as completely passive or neutral is bound to obscure the complex problems inherent in a testimony's translingual journey. Given all this, instead of restricting ourselves to merely comparing texts, we must consider the translator's real-life, real-time situation, see translators as "agents working in concrete sociological conditions" (Davies 2017, 27), and understand translation as more "a mode of interpretive reading for a specific purpose" (Davies 2017). Thus, the circumstances under which Gao worked cannot be ignored – including his particular social and cultural background, his interpretation of the survivors' life stories against that background, and his thinking about how to refashion those stories for a new Chinese audience. In leading Chinese readers to engage with the Jewish past, tension is almost inevitable between the authenticity of the encounter and its efficacy.

In trying to cross linguistic boundaries so as to achieve intercultural communication, Gao was certain to encounter inherent challenges to linguistic fidelity. What he finally produced is both an achievement and a problem. On the one hand, he clearly recognized the human suffering involved and went to great lengths to convey his sense of that to his readers. On the other hand, he failed to make the original testimony heard in its entirety, and to that extent the liberties he took and more generally his attempt to liken the Holocaust to Chinese wartime experiences cannot help but stir controversy. Gao came to take the liberties he took because his author friend had given him carte blanche, because he wanted to make the translated books both readable and elegant, because of the way he understood the translator's role as secondary witness, and possibly also because of overconfidence (i.e., the manager mentality transferred to his translator role). The inaccuracies and excessive license in his translations are bound to draw criticism for distorting the original experiences. But Gao didn't mean to "distort" his authors' life experiences. He possessed little understanding of the Holocaust and its aftermath in the West at the time he took up the translation assignment pushed by a friend. His ignorance of the status of the Holocaust in the West is relevant here. When I told Gao how sensitive the topic is and the general way of translating Holocaust memoirs in the West, he was taken aback to discover that his translation practice might be perceived as controversial.

Gao's translations may not be perfect, but he is a dedicated, well-meaning translator who has made a great contribution to the two testimonies' journey in China. He generously took the authors' suggestion of translating their books and worked hard to make them accessible to the Chinese reading public. The translations were successfully published and promoted, and enjoyed a good reception at the time. They generated the social value of Holocaust remembrance in China. The historian Annette Wieviorka observes that "the purpose of testimony is no longer to obtain knowledge ... but rather to keep them before our eyes" (1994, 24). The value of Stern's and Horak's testimonies lies more in an emotional recall of trauma than in the imparting of rigorous knowledge. It is less important whether a piece of trivial information Gao translated about their past is precisely accurate or not; what matters more is the affect and the thought they provoke in the audience. Consequently, the Chinese readers who read the two Holocaust survivors' memoirs may pass over the question of the translation's linguistic losses and gains in comparison with the originals. Instead, they will focus on addressing larger social issues such as war, humanity, and racial equality, as reflected in these works. In this way, Gao brings the survivors' harrowing experiences to a different audience and keeps those memories alive. He can be said to have effectively communicated the survivors' life stories in China and so helped to create a new Chinese remembrance of the Holocaust.

Some critics may find fault with Gao for failing to indicate explicitly the liberties he took in his translations. Although he offered ample justification for his interventionist approach in a private email to a friend, his specific take on translation was never exposed to target readers of the two testimonies. As a result, most Chinese readers, without the means for a careful textual comparison, would naturally assume everything they're reading has a counterpart in the original texts. Admittedly, Stern and Horak gave Gao a free hand and he no doubt saw himself as translating (and correcting and expanding) in the spirit of the originals. But the question remains as to whether he was justified in making substantial interventions without explicitly informing his readers. Perhaps he should have alerted his readers to his particular take on Yan Fu's three criteria, indicating that his Chinese versions of the two books constitute *adapted* translations? However, according to Peter Davies' observation regarding general translation practice, translators rarely indicate explicitly their adjustment of an original text to make it more accessible to a target audience, even though the procedure itself is common. The rationale lies in the external critical pressure often exerted on translators to adhere to the witness's own voice while at the same time listening attentively for deficiencies in the witness's text and keeping these intact as the repercussions of extreme experiences. Even so, as Davies emphasized, "it is only the explicit statement that is unusual, not the procedure itself" (2014, 177–178).

In writing about Gao's translations, I am not countenancing or defending any alteration or distortion of Holocaust material in principle, but simply reporting on what's been done and exploring the relevant circumstances. Given that most Chinese readers access Holocaust testimony in translation, we need to acknowledge the extra layer of mediation shaping their understanding. This study has revealed how Gao came to take certain liberties, why some readers may object to these, and why they might nonetheless have made sense to Gao in the specific circumstances under which he worked. Gao's translation practice offers an unusual – perhaps even extreme – case that alerts us not only to the ethical concerns surrounding the translation of Holocaust testimony but also to the need to take into account the broader sociocultural context. If we acknowledge the specific context in which Gao did his work, we can see him striving to preserve the survivors' memories under particular governing cultural conditions. A textual comparison of the original and the translation may show him as a translator taking advantage of unusual freedom, but considering the target context, we can also see Gao as both heeding and trying to preserve the primary witness by making choices and attempts that he saw as not necessarily the best but perhaps the best within the realm of what was viable. And perhaps the ultimate takeaway from all this is that any translation, whatever the translator's intent, must inevitably be a work undertaken under real-life circumstances and in real-time.

References

Adorno, Theodor W. 1967. *Prisms*. Translated by Shierry Weber Nicholsen and Samuel Weber. Cambridge, MA: The MIT Press.

Aixelá, Javier Franco. 1996. "Culture-specific items in translation." In *Translation, Power, Subversion*, edited by Román Álvarez and María Carmen-África Vidal, 52–78. Clevedon: Multilingual Matters.

Alexander, Zaia. 2007. "Primo Levi and translation." In *The Cambridge Companion to Primo Levi*, edited by Robert S. C. Gordon, 155–170. Cambridge: Cambridge University Press.

Anonymous. 2007. "集邮爱好和工作对于逃脱纳粹的魔爪居然也有如此大的作用" [Hobby and work in stamp collection could be so useful in helping him escape Nazi persecution]. Douban, December 6, comment on the Chinese translation of *My Stamp on Life*. https://book.douban.com/subject/1192840/comments/.

Anonymous. 2012. "对纳粹迫害犹太人的暴行有了切肤体会" [(Through this book I) keenly felt the suffering endured by the Jews subjected to Nazi persecution . . .]. Douban, Feburary 22, comment on the Chinese translation of *Auschwitz to Australia*. https://book.douban.com/subject/4727297/comments/.

Assmann, Aleida. 2006. "History, memory, and the genre of testimony." *Poetics Today* 27(2): 261–273.

Bakhtin, Mikhail Mikhailovich. 1996. *The Dialogic Imagination: Four Essays*. Edited by Michael Holquist. Translated by Caryl Emerson and Michael Holquist. Austin: University of Texas Press.

Batchelor, Kathryn. 2018. *Translation and Paratexts*. London: Routledge.

Bekkevold, Jo Inge. 2022. "Imperialist master, comrade in arms, foe, partner, and now ally? China's changing views of Russia." In *Russia-China Relations: Emerging Alliance or Eternal Rivals?* edited by Sarah Kirchberger, Svenja Sinjen, and Nils Wörmer, 41–58. Cham: Springer.

Bellos, David. 2022. "Translating Holocaust testimony: A translator's perspective." In *The Routledge Handbook of Translation and Memory*, edited by Sharon Deane-Cox and Anneleen Spiessens, 13–21. Oxon: Routledge.

Boase-Beier, Jean, Peter Davies, Andrea Hammel, and Marion Winters. 2017. "Introduction." In *Translating Holocaust Lives*, edited by Jean Boase-Beier, Peter Davies, Andrea Hammel, and Marion Winters, 1–21. London: Bloomsbury Academic.

References

Bodeker, Birgit. 1991. "Terms of material culture in Jack London's the call of the wild and its German translations." In *Intercutlurality and the Historical Study of Literary Translations*, edited by Harald Kittel and Armin Paul Frank, 64–70. Berlin: Erich Schmidt.

Bourdieu, Pierre. 2000. *Pascalian Meditations*. Translated by Richard Nice. Stanford, CA: Stanford University Press.

Chan, Leo Tak-hung. 2004. *Twentieth-Century Chinese Translation Theory: Modes, Issues and Debates*. Amsterdam: John Benjamins.

Davies, Peter. 2014. "Testimony and translation." *Translation and Literature* 23(2): 170–184.

Davies, Peter. 2017. "Ethics and the translation of Holocaust lives." In *Translating Holocaust Lives*, edited by Jean Boase-Beier, Peter Davies, Andrea Hammel, and Morion Winters, 23–43. London: Bloomsbury Academic.

Davies, Peter. 2018. *Witness between Languages: The Translation of Holocaust Testimonies in Context*. Rochester, NY: Camden House.

Deane-Cox, Sharon. 2013. "The translator as secondary witness: Mediating memory in Antelme's *L'espèce humaine*." *Translation Studies* 6(3): 309–323.

Du Bois, John W. 2007. "The stance triangle." In *Stancetaking in Discourse: Subjectivity, Evaluation, Interaction*, edited by Robert Englebretson, 139–182. Amsterdam: John Benjamins.

Engel, David. 2000. *The Holocaust: The Third Reich and the Jews*. Harlow: Longman.

Englebretson, Robert. 2007. "Stancetaking in discourse: An introduction." In *Stancetaking in Discourse: Subjectivity, Evaluation, Interaction*, edited by Robert Englebretson, 1–25. Amsterdam: John Benjamins.

Ezrahi, Sidra DeKoven. 1980. *By Words Alone: The Holocaust Literature*. Chicago: The University of Chicago Press.

Friedländer, Saul. 2008. *The Years of Extermination: Nazi Germany and the Jews, 1939–1945*. New York: Harper Perennial.

Gao, Shan. 2004a. 邮话连篇 [*Selections of Philatelic Research*]. Beijing: Posts and Telecom Press.

Gao, Shan. 2004b. "我所尊敬的一位外国老人——老马" [Lao Ma, an elderly foreigner whom I respect]. In Max Stern's 我的邮票生涯:集中营、大屠杀、集邮——一位幸存者的故事 [*My Stamp on Life*], translated by Gao Shan, 1–5. Beijing: Posts and Telecom Press.

Gao, Shan. 2004c. "译者后记" [The translator's afterword]. In Max Stern's 我的邮票生涯:集中营、大屠杀、集邮——一位幸存者的故事 [*My Stamp on Life*], translated by Gao Shan, 149–153. Beijing: Posts and Telecom Press.

Gao, Shan. 2010a. "序" [Preface]. In Olga Horak's 丛奥斯威辛到澳大利亚:一位纳粹大屠杀幸存者的记忆 [*Auschwitz to Australia: A Holocaust Survivor's Memoir*], translated by Gao Shan. Beijing: Posts and Telecom Press. No pages.

Gao, Shan. 2010b. "后记" [Afterword]. In Olga Horak's 丛奥斯威辛到澳大利亚:一位纳粹大屠杀幸存者的记忆 [*Auschwitz to Australia: A Holocaust Survivor's Memoir*], translated by Gao Shan, 156–163. Beijing: Posts and Telecom Press.

Gao, Shan. 2011a. "序" [Preface]. In Max Stern's 马克斯自述:成功因素——我的邮商生涯 [*The Max Factor: My Life as a Stamp Dealer*], translated by Gao Shan. Beijing: Posts and Telecom Press. No pages.

Gao, Shan. 2011b. "译者后记" [The translator's afterword]. In Max Stern's 马克斯自述:成功因素——我的邮商生涯 [*The Max Factor: My Life as a Stamp Dealer*], translated by Gao Shan, 193–195. Beijing: Posts and Telecom Press.

Genette, Gérard. 1997. *Paratexts: Thresholds of Interpretation*. Translated by Jane E. Lewin. Cambridge: Cambridge University Press.

Gramling, David. 2012. "An other unspeakability: Levi and 'Lagerszpracha.'" *New German Critique* 39(3): 165–187.

Hämäläinen, Juha, Honglin Chen, and Fang Zhao. 2017. "The Chinese welfare philosophy in light of the traditional concept of family." *International Social Work* 62(1): 224–239.

Hanna, Sameh. 2016. *Bourdieu in Translation Studies: The Socio-Cultural Dynamics of Shakespeare Translation in Egypt*. New York: Routledge.

Hass, Aaron. 1995. *The Aftermath: Living with the Holocaust*. Cambridge: Cambridge University Press.

Hermans, Theo. 2014a. "Positioning translators: Voices, views and values in translation." *Language and Literature* 23(3): 285–301.

Hermans, Theo. 2014b. *The Conference of the Tongues*. London: Routledge.

Hermans, Theo. 2022. *Translation and History: A Textbook*. Abingdon: Routledge.

Hirsch, Marianne and Leo Spitzer. 2009. "The witness in the archive: Holocaust studies/ memory studies." *Memory Studies* 2(2): 151–170.

Holquist, Michael. 1990. *Dialogism: Bakhtin and His World*. London: Routledge.

Horak, Olga. 2000. *Auschwitz to Australia: A Holocaust Survivor's Memoir*. Sydney: Kangaroo Press.

Horak, Olga. 2010. 从奥斯威辛集中营到澳大利亚:一位纳粹大屠杀幸存者的记忆 [*Auschwitz to Australia: A Holocaust Survivor's Memoir*]. Translated by Gao Shan. Beijing: Posts and Telecom Press.

Insana, Lina N. 2009. *Arduous Tasks: Primo Levi, Translation, and the Transmission of Holocaust Testimony*. Toronto: University of Toronto Press.

References

Jaffe, Alexandra. 2009. *Stance: Sociolinguistic Perspectives*. New York: Oxford University Press.

Kärkkäinen, Elise. 2006. "Stancetaking in conversation: From subjectivity to intersubjectivity." *Text & Talk – An Interdisciplinary Journal of Language, Discourse & Communication Studies* 26(6): 699–731.

Kiesling, Scott Fabius, Umashanthi Pavalanathan, Jim Fitzpatrick, Xiaochuang Han, and Jacob Eisenstein. 2018. "Interactional stance-taking in online forums." *Computational Linguistics* 44(4): 683–718.

Kiesling, Scott F. 2022. "Stance and stancetaking." *Annual Reviews of Linguistics* 8(1): 409–426.

Laub, Dori. 1992a. "Bearing witness, or the vicissitudes of listening." In *Testimony: Crises of Witnessing in Literature, Psychoanalysis, and History*, edited by Shoshana Felman and Dori Laub, 57–74. London: Routledge.

Laub, Dori. 1992b. "An event without a witness: Truth, testimony and survival." In *Testimony: Crises of Witnessing in Literature, Psychoanalysis, and History*, edited by Shoshana Felman and Dori Laub, 75–92. London: Routledge.

Levi, Primo. 1959. *If This Is a Man*. Translated by Stuart Woolf. London: The Orion Press.

Levi, Primo. 1987. *If This Is a Man and the Truce*. Translated by Stuart Woolf. London: Abacus.

Levi, Primo. 1989. *The Drowned and the Saved*. Translated by Raymond Rosenthal. New York: Vintage International.

Levi, Primo. 2003. "On translating and being translated." Translated by Zaia Alexander. *Los Angeles Times*. Published March 30. www.latimes.com/archives/la-xpm-2003-mar-30-bk-levi30-story.html.

Levy, Daniel and Natan Sznaider. 2006. *The Holocaust and Memory in the Global Age*. Philadelphia, PA: Temple University Press.

Li, Mingjiang and Angela Poh. 2019. "The indispensable partner: Russia in China's grand strategy." In *Sino-Russian Relations in the 21st Century*, edited by Jo Inge Bekkevold and Bobo Lo, 21–41. Cham: Palgrave Macmillan.

Li, Sha. 2005. "二战期间曾有5名中国人惨死纳粹奥地利集中营" [Five Chinese died in a Nazi concentration camp in Austria during World War II]. 法治晚报 [*Legal Affairs Evening News*]. Published January 27. http://mil.news.sina.com.cn/2005-01-27/1346262145.html.

Lin, Yutang. 1972. *Lin Yutang's Chinese-English Dictionary of Modern Usage*. Hong Kong: The Chinese Univeristy of Hong Kong Press.

Murtisari, Elisabet Titik. 2016. "Explicitation in translation studies: The journey of an elusive concept." *Translation & Interpreting* 8(2): 64–81.

References

Neather, Robert. 2022. "Debating Buddhist translations in cyberspace: The Buddhist online discussion forum as a discursive and epitextual space." In *Unsettling Translation*, edited by Mona Baker, 197–216. Abingdon: Routledge.

O'Shea, Paul. 2000. "Foreword." In Olga Horak's *Auschwitz to Australia: A Holocaust Survivor's Memoir*, xi–xii. Sydney: Kangaroo Press.

O'Shea, Paul. 2010. "前言" [Foreword]. In Olga Horak's 从奥斯威辛集中营到澳大利亚:一位纳粹大屠杀幸存者的记忆 [*Auschwitz to Australia: A Holocaust Survivor's Memoir*], translated by Gao Shan. Beijing: The Posts and Telecom Press. No pages.

Reilly, James. 2012. *Strong Society, Smart State: The Rise of Public Opinion in China's Japan Policy*. New York: Columbia University Press.

Robinson, Andrew. 2011. "In theory: Bakhtin: Dialogism, polyphony and heteroglossia." *Ceasefire*. Published July 29. https://ceasefiremagazine.co.uk/in-theory-bakhtin-1/.

Roskies, David. 1984. *Against the Apocalypse*. Cambridge, MA: Harvard University Press.

Schmidt, Carmen. 2016. "A comparison of civil religion and remembrance culture in Germany and Japan." *Asian Journal of German and European Studies* 1(10): 1–22.

Seidman, Naomi. 1996. "Elie Wiesel and the scandal of Jewish rage." *Jewish Social Studies* 3(1): 1–19.

St. André, James. 2018. "Consequences of the conflation of *xiao* and filial piety in English." *Translation and Interpreting Studies* 13(2): 293–316.

Steiner, George. 1976. *Language and Silence: Essays on Language, Literature, and the Inhuman*. New York: Atheneum.

Stern, Max. 2003. *My Stamp on Life*. Melbourne: Makor Jewish Community Library.

Stern, Max. 2004. 我的邮票生涯:集中营、大屠杀、集邮——一位幸存者的故事 [*My Stamp on Life*]. Translated by Gao Shan. Beijing: The Posts and Telecom Press.

Stumm, Bettina. 2010. "Testifying to the infinity of the other: The sacred and ethical dimensions of secondary witnessing in Anne Karpf's *The War After*." In *Through a Glass Darkly: Suffering, the Sacred, and the Sublime in Literature and Theory*, edited by Holly Faith Nelson, Lynn R. Szabo, and Jens Zimmermann, 349–362. Waterloo: Wilfrid Laurier University Press.

Venuti, Lawrence. 1998. *The Scandals of Translation: Towards an Ethics of Difference*. London: Routledge.

Voloshinov, Valentin Nikolaevich/Mikhail Mikhailovich Bakhtin. 1983. "Discourse in life and discourse in poetry." In *Bakhtin School Papers*, translated by John Richmond, edited by Ann Shukman, 5–25. Oxford: RPT.

Wiesel, Elie. 2008. *Night*. Translated by Marion Wiesel. London: Penguin Books.

Wieviorka, Annette. 1994. "On testimony." In *Holocaust Remembrance: The Shapes of Memory*, edited by Geoffrey Hartman, 23–32. Oxford: Basil Blakwell.

Wilson, Jeanne L. 2004. *Strategic Partners: Russian-Chinese Relations in the Post-Soviet Era*. New York: M. E. Sharpe.

Wolf, Michaela. 2010. "Sociology of translation." In *Handbook of Translation Studies*, edited by Yves Gambrier and Luc van Doorslaer, 337–343. Amsterdam: John Benjamins.

Yan, Fu 2004. "Preface to Tianyanlun." In Leo Tak-hung Chan's *Twentieth-Century Chinese Translation Theory: Modes, Issues and Debates*, translated by C. Y. Hsu, 69–71. Amsterdam: John Benjamins.

Yan, Fu. 1933. "译例言" [Preface to Tianyanlun]. In T. H. Huxley's 天演论 [*Evolution and Ethics*], translated by Yan Fu, 1–3. Shanghai: Commercial Press.

Yuan, Xi. 2005. "人生的印迹" [The stamp of life]. 人民日报 [*People's Daily*]. Published January 9. Page 8. https://news.sina.com.cn/o/2005-01-09/05484763303s.shtml.

Yuan, Xi. 2010. "传递教训与启示:《从奥斯威辛集中营到澳大利亚》的作者和译者" [Passing on lessons and insights: The author and the translator of *Auschwitz to Australia*]. 人民日报 [*People's Daily*]. Published March 19. Page 19. www.chinanews.com.cn/cul/news/2010/03-19/2179078.shtml.

Zhang, Aaron. 2021. "'China Hwang' of the Nazi camp for women." *The Times of Israel*, April 9. https://blogs.timesofisrael.com/china-hwang-of-the-nazi-camp-for-women/.

Zhang, Shengzhen. 2024. "Anne Frank in China: Translation, adaptation, and reception." *International Research in Children's Literature* 17(2): 219–232.

Acknowledgments

I would like to express my gratitude to the protagonist translator of this project, Mr. Gao Shan, for the extensive information he provided me and for permission to reproduce relevant parts of those materials. Without his generosity and openness, I could not have understood the many hidden complexities of this case's texts and contexts.

I'm grateful to Olga Horak, one of the two Holocaust survivor authors, her daughter Susie Berk, as well as Sam Seigel, son-in-law of the other Holocaust survivor author Max Stern, from Max Stern & Co., for their encouragement and help in many ways. Nothing is more invaluable for this kind of project than the personal support of the Holocaust survivor and their family.

It was a privilege to work on this research at the Center for Translation Studies, UCL. I would like to thank Professor Kathryn Batchelor for facilitating my stay there. I am particularly indebted to Professor Theo Hermans for his willingness to be my mentor, and for his guidance and critical remarks on this project.

My thanks also go to my American friends Professor Leon Chai for his pertinent academic advice on my research and Ms. Cara Ryan for her help in copy-editing my manuscript.

Cambridge Elements

Translation and Interpreting

The series is edited by Kirsten Malmkjær with Sabine Braun as associate editor for Elements focusing on Interpreting.

Kirsten Malmkjær
University of Leicester

Kirsten Malmkjær is Professor Emeritus of Translation Studies at the University of Leicester. She has taught Translation Studies at the universities of Birmingham, Cambridge, Middlesex and Leicester and has written extensively on aspects of both the theory and practice of the discipline. *Translation and Creativity* (London: Routledge) was published in 2020 and *The Cambridge Handbook of Translation*, which she edited, was published in 2022. She is preparing a volume entitled *Introducing Translation* for the Cambridge Introductions to Language and Linguistics series.

Editorial Board
Adriana Serban, *Université Paul Valéry*
Barbara Ahrens, *Technische Hochschule Köln*
Liu Min-Hua, *Hong Kong Baptist University*
Christine Ji, *The University of Sydney*
Jieun Lee, *Ewha Womans University*
Lorraine Leeson, *The University of Dublin*
Sara Laviosa, *Università Delgi Stuidi di Bari Aldo Moro*
Fabio Alves, *FALE-UFMG*
Moira Inghilleri, *University of Massachusetts Amherst*
Akiko Sakamoto, *University of Portsmouth*
Haidee Kotze, *Utrecht University*

About the Series
Elements in Translation and Interpreting present cutting edge studies on the theory, practice and pedagogy of translation and interpreting. The series also features work on machine learning and AI, and human-machine interaction, exploring how they relate to multilingual societies with varying communication and accessibility needs, as well as text-focused research.

Cambridge Elements

Translation and Interpreting

Elements in the Series

Translation as Experimentalism
Tong King Lee

Translation and Genre
B. J. Woodstein

On-Screen Language in Video Games
Mikołaj Deckert and Krzysztof W. Hejduk

Navigating the Web
Claire Y. Shih

The Graeco-Arabic Translation Movement
El-Hussein AY Aly

Interpreting as Translanguaging
Lili Han, Zhisheng (Edward) Wen and Alan James Runcieman

Creative Classical Translation
Paschalis Nikolaou

Translation as Creative–Critical Practice
Delphine Grass

Translation in Analytic Philosophy
Francesca Ervas

Towards Game Translation User Research
Mikołaj Deckert, Krzysztof W. Hejduk, and Miguel Á. Bernal-Merino

Hypertranslation
Mª Carmen África Vidal Claramonte and Tong King Lee

An Extraordinary Chinese Translation of Holocaust Testimony
Meiyuan Zhao

A full series listing is available at: www.cambridge.org/EITI